D1596821

JOHN LOCKE AND THE THEORY OF SOVEREIGNTY

Cambridge Studies in the History and Theory of Politics

JOHN LOCKE AND THE THEORY OF SOVEREIGNTY

Mixed Monarchy and the Right of Resistance in the Political Thought of the English Revolution

JULIAN H. FRANKLIN

CAMBRIDGE UNIVERSITY PRESS

CAMBRIDGE

LONDON · NEW YORK · MELBOURNE

Published by the Syndics of the Cambridge University Press
The Pitt Building, Trumpington Street, Cambridge CB2 IRP
Bentley House, 200 Euston Road, London NW1 2DB
32 East 57th Street, New York, NY 10022, USA
296 Beaconsfield Parade, Middle Park, Melbourne 3206, Australia

First published 1978

Printed in Great Britain by
Western Printing Services Ltd, Bristol

Library of Congress Cataloguing in Publication Data
Franklin, Julian H.
John Locke and the theory of sovereignty
(Cambridge studies in the history and
theory of politics)
Bibliography: p.
Includes index.
1. Sovereignty. 2. Monarchy. 3. Locke,
John, 1632–1704. 4. Great Britain – History – Stuarts,
1603–1714 I. Title.
JC327.F7 1978 321.8'7 77–80833
ISBN 0 521 21758 X

To the memory of my father, Jerome A. Franklin

CONTENTS

PREFACE

My purpose in this study is to describe and explain a fundamental transformation in the theory of sovereignty which
entered the modern tradition via Locke. In the standard
constitutionalist theory of the late sixteenth and early seventeenth centuries, the ultimate right of a people to depose a king
for tyranny and to alter the powers of his office was normally
equated with the rights of constituted bodies established as the
people's representative. In this form, the principle of popular
sovereignty was incompatible with the partial independence of
the king in the normal workings of a mixed or limited
monarchy. At the beginning of the English civil wars, in 1642,
the attempts of Parliamentary theorists to combine recognition
of the king's independence with a right of resistance in the
Parliament led to manifold and deep confusion.

The resolution of these difficulties was the work of George
Lawson, a political moderate writing in the later Interregnum.
In Lawson's view the legal consequences, in 1642, of the conflict between king and Parliament, was an entire dissolution of
the government and reversion of power to the people, which
was alone entitled to constitute a new authority. Ultimate
sovereignty – in the sense of constituent authority – was thus
denied to Parliament and ascribed to the general community
as a legal entity distinct from Parliament. In his *Politica sacra
et civilis*, Lawson reworked the entire theory of sovereignty in
the light of this conception. This work, in my opinion, is
among the deepest treatments of this subject in his century.

Lawson's theory was to be neglected in the 1680s, in large
part because its implications seemed too radical. But his idea of

dissolution was taken up by Locke, whose adherence to this new conception provides us with a deeper understanding of his intellectual and political intentions as well as his stature as a political theorist. Although the theory of dissolution, as it was presented in the *Second Treatise*, was deliberately rejected by almost all his Whig contemporaries, Locke held fast to his position. He had found, and knew that he had found, the only adequate solution to the problem of resistance in a mixed constitution. It was, indeed, a solution to the problem of sovereignty in any constitution whatsoever, as well as a formula for the change of institutions by an independent act of the community. And it was perhaps for these reasons, more than any other, that the *Second Treatise* was belatedly received as a classic of modern constitutionalism.

A brief summary of the general theme of this book was presented to the Iowa Humanities Society in 1975. Parts of chapter 3 were included in a paper delivered at the 1976 Convention of the American Political Science Association and the Columbia University Seminar for the Study of Political and Social Thought. These opportunities to gauge reactions and receive suggestions were much appreciated. The manuscript was completed during the academic year 1975–6 with the help of a grant from the National Endowment for the Humanities.

Among the many individuals who gave me advice, criticism, and encouragement at various stages of my work are Ralph E. Giesey, Douglas Hodgson, Donald R. Kelley, J. G. A. Pocock, J. H. M. Salmon, and Eileen P. Sullivan. I am especially grateful for the judicious appraisal and encouragement I received from Abraham Ascher, and I am indebted to Herbert A. Deane for his careful reading and discerning comments. In revising the manuscript for publication, I profited greatly from several conversations with Quentin Skinner, whose criticisms were always to the point and generously constructive. I wish to thank my wife, Paula A. Franklin, for her editorial help and for managing to maintain her patience.

All translations are my own unless otherwise indicated. The titles of seventeenth-century works have often been shortened. I have also modernized orthography and punctuation wherever I thought the original form might be distracting to the reader. The one exception is Locke's *Two Treatises*. Here I have strictly followed Laslett's text, which has now become standard and familiar. For speeches and statements in Parliament I have regularly cited Cobbett's *Parliamentary History of England* which, for most readers, will be the most convenient and readily available source. But for many citations I have included alternative references in parentheses.

I
The background of the problem

IN THE COURSE of the English civil wars a new dimension was added to the constitutionalist theory of sovereignty which entered the main tradition through the work of Locke. In the last chapter of the *Second Treatise*, entitled 'Of the Dissolution of Government,' Locke insists on the right of the people, acting for just cause, not only to replace its governors but to change the form of government itself. By the people, furthermore, he does not mean the Parliament, or even the House of Commons within Parliament, but the general political community considered as a separate legal entity. This idea seemed radical at the time it was published, and was repudiated by the Whigs. But it did not originate in any particular zeal for political democracy. In the form in which Locke encountered it, and as he used it, it seemed to be the only principle of resistance consistent with the relationships of sovereignty in a mixed constitution.

In earlier constitutionalist theory, which had attained definitive elaboration in the monarchomach writers of the sixteenth century, the right of resistance and of deposition had also been based on the constituent power of the people. Since all legitimate authority derived from the consent of the community and was thereby subject to conditions, the people had the right to depose a king if these conditions were flagrantly transgressed.[1]

[1] The basic themes of monarchomach theory are treated in many places. My own view is presented in Julian H. Franklin, *Constitutionalism and Resistance in the Sixteenth Century* (New York, 1969).

For general surveys of European political thought in this period, see J. W. Allen, *Political Thought in the Sixteenth Century* (London, 1957);

But in this monarchomach tradition, the constituent power of the people was almost always equated with the right of the Three Estates or other body in which the people were considered to be represented. In other words, the right of the people's representative and that of the general community were assumed to be legally equivalent and interchangeable – by substitution, as it were.[2] Hence the right of the Estates to act against a tyrant was thought to be inherent in their capacity as representatives, and the original contract by which the king was constituted was portrayed as an act of the Estates on behalf of the community.

Among most of the best known monarchomachs, indeed, the very constitution of the people as a corporate association was in the form of an Estates assembly. Given the fear of democratic revolution in this period, this interpretation rapidly became predominant. The right of resistance could be confined to the established representative, and, where the Estates were incapable of acting, to the higher magistrates and nobles of the kingdom whom the Estates had supposedly instituted to restrain the king on their behalf. Initiation of resistance by ordinary subjects, and so by the populace at large, was forbidden as antisocial and anarchic.

Yet even those who admitted individual initiative did not

and Pierre Mesnard, *L'essor de la philosophie politique au XVI⁰ siècle* (2nd ed. Paris, 1951). Still lacking is a detailed and comprehensive study not so much of the 'systems' of individual thinkers as of the main intellectual trends as they develop in response to political issues and institutional changes. But that need will soon be fully supplied by Quentin Skinner in his forthcoming book, *The Foundations of Modern Political Thought*, 2 vols. (Cambridge, 1978).

[2] The assumption of full substitution is especially articulate in the *Vindiciae contra tyrannos*. And it is used to describe not only the Estates but the magistrates who are assumed to hold of the Estates either by election or a tenure created by the Estates in the past. 'When we speak of the people collectively, we mean those who receive authority from the people, that is, the magistrates below the king who have been elected by the people or established in some other way. Those take the place of the people assembled as a whole and are ephors to kings and associates in their rule. And we also mean the assembly of the Estates, which are nothing less than the epitome of a kingdom to which all public matters are referred.' (Franklin, *Constitutionalism*, p. 149.)

intend thereby that freedom to act by the Estates should be restricted. Individual acts of tyrannicide, or a rising by ordinary subjects, were but remedies of last resort, when the Estates were unwilling or unable to take action, and the higher magistrates and nobles had failed to do their duty.[3] Hence the right of the Estates to act against a tyrant as the people's substitute was the common assumption of all constitutionalist commentators.[4]

Thus understood, however, the right of deposition was technically incompatible with a mixed or limited monarchy. In a limited monarchy the king, although circumscribed by law, has a legal monopoly of all constitutional initiatives; in a mixed monarchy constitutional initiative is shared by the king and the Estates. In either form the king is vested with a large sphere of independent power which the representative body must be forbidden to assume.[5] Where the Estates hold constituent authority, however, no such independence is allowable.

[3] Appeal to individual resistance in first instance was sometimes allowed by medieval writers. But this had been regarded by most as dangerously anarchic. With the growth of representative institutions, individual resistance (when admitted at all) tends to be reduced to the status of a last resort.

[4] The only exception to this rule is George Buchanan, *De jure regni apud Scotos* (1578), in *Opera Omnia* (Edinburgh, 1715), vol. I, who holds (p. 13) that acts of the Estates do not obtain the force of law unless they have been ratified by the (tacit) consent of the general community. There is thus some conception in Buchanan of the people as a corporate entity distinct from the Estates, and having powers of its own. I am indebted to Quentin Skinner for calling this point to my attention.

Buchanan, however, does not deny the rights of the Estates to substitute for the people in all respects so long, presumably, as their acts were not flagrantly neglectful of the public interest. That this substitution by the Estates also extended to the constituent functions of creating and deposing kings is clearly indicated by many passages in Buchanan's slightly later work, *The History of Scotland* (1582), trans. J. Fraser (London, 1689). See especially I, 114, 269, 331; and II, 215, 216, 222.

[5] This distinction between limited and mixed is presented from a modern point of view. Most European writers, in so far as they are able to recognize an independent but qualified kingship, do not distinguish different modes. The distinction between limited and mixed is embryonic in many English writers of the seventeenth century and these terms are used by Philip Hunton (see below, pp. 41ff.). But Hunton's distinction does not exactly correspond to the one offered here.

Since the powers of the king are granted to him on condition, he is obliged to use them in the public interest. And if the Estates have all the powers of the principal by which that agency was constituted, there can be no power in the king that restricts their scope of judgment. The deliberate opinion of the Estates, when actually assembled, must define the public interest authoritatively.

In monarchomach theory, then, there was no sphere of public power that the Estates could not assume. Thus in all European monarchies the power of declaring war was wholly or partly vested in the king. But if, in a given situation, the Estates were assembled and requested war, the king would be obliged to yield, even against his better judgment. This would apply to every other area of executive and legislative power, for on the premise we have just described all powers of the king had to be temporarily suspended in the presence of the assembled representative. The same consideration can be stated in another way. A king could not presume to refuse, or veto, a persistent request of the Estates, or order them dissolved against their will, without appearing to assert that his power to define the public interest was unconditional and arbitrary. A king who adopted such a course would *eo ipso* be culpable of tyranny, and he would become liable to resistance or removal by those who had granted him his office.

The monarchomach theorists do not always stress this outcome, and often write of any given monarchy as though it were limited or mixed.[6] But all of them, at some point or another,

---

[6] Thus François Hotman, in the *Francogallia*, puts the entire control of public affairs in the Estates Assembly and thinks of the king as properly but the presiding officer therein (Franklin, *Constitutionalism*, pp. 71, 73). Yet he lavishly praises the French constitution as a 'mixture' (*ibid*. pp. 66–8). 'Mixture' is thus not used in a strictly legal sense but only to show that the government of France is somehow composed of three elements cooperating harmoniously. A strict juridical distinction between the sharing of sovereignty and the sharing of subsidiary governmental functions by several components is introduced only with Bodin, who denies the possibility of the former while admitting the latter. But even after Bodin the confusion lingers on. See Julian H. Franklin, *Jean Bodin and the Rise of Absolutist Theory* (Cambridge, 1973), pp. 29ff.

explicitly observe or clearly imply that the assembled representative can assume all the powers of the central government whenever it sees need to do so.[7] The essence of monarchy, in the monarchomach perspective, is the right of the king to govern in conformity with law when the representative is not in session. Since the Estates of the sixteenth century were not assembled continuously or even frequently, there is a certain common sense in this idea of monarchy, and it could go hand in hand with a large degree of effective power in the king. Yet in strict juridical terms, the king in this conception is not an

---

[7] This tendency is beautifully illustrated by the following passage from Johannes Althusius, whose *Politica methodice digesta* is the academic *summa* of monarchomach thought. 'Therefore, the estates and orders taken together prevails over the opinion of the presiding officer or supreme magistrate. For there is more authority and power in a group of many persons than in one individual who has been constituted by that group of many and is inferior to them. Several persons can understand, see, and judge better than one; and one is more likely than many to err and be deceived, or to be driven by his passions into wrongful acts. What many seek is more readily found, and what has been decided by the authority of many is observed and maintained with greater harmony, authority, and good faith. Furthermore, if the magistrate's own opinion, being opposed to the opinion of the orders and estates taken both separately and together, should be promulgated as the opinion of the general council, the council would be meeting in vain. The example of Theodosius is presented in *l. humanum. C. de legib.* [Code 1, 14, 8] where that pious Emperor says that general law is to be that only which has been approved by the common consent of all and the council of all estates together and then promulgated by the Emperor's authority...On the authority of councils there is much to be found in Hotman, the *Antimachiavel* [Gentillet],...and Bodin, who does not believe, however, that the decrees of assemblies are valid and ratified unless they are approved by the king...But in modern times all difficulty [on this question] is removed by the articles, sworn to by the king at the time of his installation, in which he promises that he will do nothing in important matters without the council of the kingdom's leading men' (*Politica methodice digesta* (Cambridge, Mass., 1932), ch. XXXIII, 20, pp. 32–4).

As this passage indicates, the obligation of the king to obtain the consent of an assembly is not distinguished from an obligation to follow its advice, and evidence of the first is taken to indicate the second also. This error is widespread in the period and is found among absolutists as well, who, of course, often use it for different purposes. On Bodin, see Franklin, *Bodin*, p. 68. For Pufendorf, see *On the Law of Nature and Nations*, trans. C. H. and W. A. Oldfather (Oxford, 1934), VII, ch. VI, 12, p. 1076.

independent power. He is better described as an agent charged by the Estates, who is bound to carry out their will and holds office during good behavior.

The monarchomach theory of resistance was thus at odds with existing constitutional realities. But the specific difficulty was never pointed out by its opponents. Those who rallied to the prince's side in the conflicts of the time were unwilling to defend their cause on the premise of limited supremacy.[8] The aim of the royalists was to invalidate resistance altogether; to acknowledge binding limitations on the king was to admit that resistance in some form or other must be licit if these limits were transgressed. In the sixteenth century, accordingly, and in the seventeenth as well, the royalist argument tended to be absolutist, and was as much, or more, at odds with constitutional realities as the doctrine it attempted to refute.

On the other hand, those who took up arms against the king were never driven to reassess their theory of monarchy in response to pressures from within their ranks. The monarchomach doctrine of resistance was no doubt republican in tendency. But this did not become a source of political embarrassment.[9] In the organized resistance movements of the time, the idea of an aristocratic republic with a princely chief often seemed a congenial solution to their grievances. And we have already seen that they were not required logically to press their claims to that extreme. Their actual demands for day-to-

[8] This is mainly true of royalist thought on the continent. The English royalist position of the 1640s is more complex. See below, pp. 34ff.

[9] In all monarchomach theories the normal and continuing checks on the king are the high nobles and corps of magistrates like the Parlement of Paris whose power is to limit rather than control the king (except when they initiate resistance). In some versions, as in the *Vindiciae contra tyrannos*, the emphasis on these 'lesser magistrates' beneath the king is so great as to eclipse the role of the Estates. Generally speaking, the right of the Estates, or people, is usually little more than a general principle to explain the right of resistance in the magistrates. The theory of these magistrates – who are virtually independent powers in the monarchomach theory of the state – is lucidly worked out in the first part of Richard Roy Benert, 'Inferior Magistrates in Sixteenth Century Political and Legal Thought,' unpublished doctoral dissertation, University of Minnesota, 1967.

day control of affairs by the Estates could be expanded or
contracted in any given situation without alteration of the basic
premise on which their theory of resistance was established. In
the sixteenth century, accordingly, the inability of constitutionalist theory to account for a limited or mixed monarchy
was passed over virtually unnoticed.

But at the time of the English civil wars, which began in
1642, the entire question of resistance was transformed. For
reasons soon to be considered, the leaders of the English opposition were unwilling to claim a right of deposition against
Charles I, and strenuously denied that such a right existed.
They attempted, rather, to justify a war against the king while
still acknowledging his title and authority. As a result of this
decision, the incompatibility, characteristic of the older theory,
between the ultimate supremacy of the people's representative
and the independence of the king, was transformed into a
contradiction in the theory itself. The leaders of the opposition
were conceding that a king of England was somehow independent in his status. But in order to justify resistance, they were
required, in one way or another, to invoke the supremacy of
Parliament against him.

Sooner or later, then, despite all efforts at evasion, this
fundamental inconsistency would have to be noted, not only
by the royalists, but by the constitutionalists themselves. It thus
prepared the way, in some of these at least, for a reconstruction
of the theory of sovereignty. Given the attachment of the
English to the principle of royal independence, return to
monarchomach conceptions was no longer feasible. The only
reasonable solution to the problem of resistance was the location
of constituent authority in the people as distinct from Parliament.

The theoretical difficulties of the Parliamentary position in
the early 1640s did not result, at least initially, from any
particular concern to preserve the balance of the English constitution. They were engendered rather by a compromise in
political strategy. The dominant aim of the Parliamentary
leadership was to guarantee the constitution against any new

attempt by Charles I to rule without a Parliament. In the first half of 1641 the Long Parliament, which had been convened in November 1640, passed a number of important measures that seemed sufficient to achieve these goals.[10] These proposals had become law with Charles' consent. But since Charles could not be trusted personally, no guarantees were calculated to give real assurance, short of virtually complete control of the entire executive establishment, to which Charles would not agree.[11] By the time of the Irish rebellion that began in October 1641, the leaders of the opposition had become fully persuaded that Charles was planning a military coup against the Parliament, and they now began to prepare their supporters in and out of Parliament for civil war. At this point it might seem that their only sensible course was deposition. If Charles could not be trusted, and if he would not consent to surrender his control of the executive, there was no security for Parliament unless he were driven from the throne.

But the majority of the House of Commons, to say nothing of the Lords, were as much or even more alarmed by the revolutionary menace attendant on protracted civil war, as by the threat from Charles. In France, and even in the Low Countries, the military resistance of the sixteenth century had centered, at least initially, on the fighting nobles of the countryside. The towns made financial contributions that were often used to hire mercenaries and to pay for the importation of auxiliaries. But the core of the resistance effort normally lay in clienteles

[10] Among these were the Triennial Act, the Act of Continuance (by which the Long Parliament could not be dissolved without its own consent) and the dismantling of the prerogative courts.
[11] Charles was repeatedly asked to appoint and retain such officers and counsellors as enjoyed the confidence of Parliament. This demand, which is almost constant, became more specific, all-encompassing, and insistent as the conflict deepened. A fairly early and relatively mild statement is a resolution adopted by the House of Commons on June 23, 1641 'that his majesty may be humbly petitioned to remove such evil counsellors against whom there be any just exception, and for the committing of his own business and the affairs of the kingdom to such counsellors and officers as the Parliament may have cause to confide in...' (William Cobbett (ed.), *Parliamentary History of England*, vol. II (London, 1807), col. 847).

of local nobles attached to great princes or to local magnates with national, or even international, connections. In England, on the other hand, the rural fighting noble and the network of quasi-feudal clienteles had long been obsolescent. The English opposition, furthermore, was unique among European resistance movements in that it clearly centered in a House of Commons. And in part for this reason, what quasi-feudal elements remained tended to rally to the cause of Charles. By 1641, indeed, there were serious defections from the House of Lords to join the king when he departed London. Many who left had been virtually driven from the city by the crowds that had been used, or at least permitted, by the House of Commons to intimidate the other House.

Hence any Parliamentary army, although it might be led by gentlemen and sympathetic Lords, would have to recruit its rank-and-file – and many of its officers too, as it turned out – from social strata not represented in the House of Commons. It would thus be drawn from artisans and yeomen, numbers of whom attended congregations illegally separated from the state in which sectarian radicalism often flourished. And this sectarianism often went hand in hand with alarming notions of political and social revolution. In all the great European conflicts occasioned by the Reformation, the official resistance inevitably inspired, and sometimes exploited, radicalism of this sort. But the continental radicalism of the sixteenth century had most often been inchoate, naive, and easily kept on the fringes of the military struggle. In England of the seventeenth century the radicals were better organized and often quite sophisticated in their ideas of secular reform; above all, they could not be easily excluded from the army. As the most eager and most militant members of the strata from which it was recruited, they could hardly be denied participation, even though attempts were made to do so.[12]

The official Parliamentary opposition was thus inclined to

---

[12] See Christopher Hill, *God's Englishman, Oliver Cromwell and the English Revolution* (New York, 1972), ch. III.

9

caution. In 1640 its leaders believed, or affected to believe, that their constitutional objectives could be accomplished short of war. They could hardly have done otherwise and kept their majority together.[13] During the 'paper war' of 1642 – which took the form of Remonstrances and Addresses by the Parliament on the one side, Answers to remonstrances and addresses by the king on the other, and Declarations by both, all designed to win support among the public – both the rank-and-file of the moderate opposition, and probably the leadership as well, hoped that Charles would finally yield to a determined threat of military force. Even after August 1642, when Charles was artfully maneuvered into the first open breach of civil peace, they believed that the war could be ended speedily by compromise. In 1645, Charles was defeated after a bitter and protracted struggle. But by this point the official opposition had even greater reason to insist that he was still the king. Threatened with the growth of radicalism in the army, its members pressed for a negotiated settlement before the menace could mature. They clung to this strategy tenaciously, until the more moderate wing was driven from the House of Commons in the military purge of December 1648.

Hence at no point, so long as it was free, did the Long Parliament move toward deposition, or even think of it, at least officially. The closest that it came was the Vote of No Addresses of January 1648, which declared that the two houses would settle the constitution unilaterally in view of Charles' obstinacy. Even this preliminary step was but a momentary and half-hearted deviation.

Throughout the 1640s, therefore, Parliament was bound to insist on the sacrosanctity of Charles, not only in his person but also in his official status. Having repeatedly declared the existence of a grand conspiracy centering on Charles, to subvert the constitution and to introduce an arbitrary government, Parliament could hardly say that Charles was morally innocent

[13] See Jack H. Hexter, *The Reign of King Pym* (Cambridge, Mass., 1961), ch. 1.

of tyrannical behavior and intent. It could justify its failure to depose only by disclaiming any right to do so. Hence one component in its legal theory, and the inconsistency that it thus embraced, was the English maxim that a king can do no wrong. For all acts done by Charles which the Parliament held to be illegal, only his instruments and counsellors were legally responsible! Charles himself, on the other hand, was not accountable in law, and could not be punished in his person or removed from office. Hence Parliament was implicitly conceding that a king of England had to be sovereign at least in some respect. If he could not be held accountable by Parliament, he must possess a sphere of power that was independent of the Parliament and which it could not touch.

Yet at the same time Parliament, in prosecuting civil war, would raise an army, levy taxes, and assume general executive authority without the king's consent. In order to justify this course, it was forced – albeit with reluctance and embarrassment – to set forth legal claims that amounted, sometimes almost on their face, to assertions of constituent authority. The high point of such claims was the defense of the Militia Ordinance passed by the two houses in the spring of 1642. This measure was the first decisive step by Parliament toward civil war, and the first assertion of the right to legislate without the king. The attempt to demonstrate this right in the paper war of 1642 was also the one occasion when Parliament itself attempted to articulate the grounds on which all subsequent measures required for the civil war were based.

The political aim of the Militia Ordinance, which was enacted by the two houses in early March 1642, was to forestall any military coup by depriving Charles of all command over domestic military forces. By the terms of the ordinance, the militia and fortifications of the several counties were entrusted to lieutenant generals particularly mentioned in the act. The persons named were given full command, until such time as the act should be rescinded, except as they should 'receive directions by his majesty's authority signified unto them by the

Lords and Commons assembled in Parliament.'[14] We shall later see that this formula meant command by Parliament alone. The intent of the Militia Ordinance was to create an army that Charles could not control.

The leaders of the opposition had little reason to expect that the act would be certified by Charles as law. This was the reason why the act was passed not as a bill but as an 'ordinance.'[15] The very term suggested unilateral action since it had been used in English law only for binding proclamations enacted by the king alone. Indeed, in Parliament's contention the Militia Ordinance acquired all the force of law as soon as it had passed both houses on March 5, 1642.[16] But if only for the sake of form, or propaganda, Charles was repeatedly petitioned to give the ordinance his royal approbation. After much haggling for public effect, and several declarations on either side, Charles' initial demurrer became a final refusal, and he declared the ordinance to be utterly void.[17] On May 5, 1642, the two houses responded by declaring that the ordinance was finally in execution.[18]

Of the two main arguments put forward to justify this course, one was a theory of legislation belatedly discovered by the Parliament in the royal oath of coronation. According to a version of the oath that appeared in a statute passed under Edward III, a king of England was sworn to keep, protect, and confirm the 'justas leges et consuetudines. . .quas vulgus

---

[14] Cobbett, vol. ii, col. 1084 (or John Rushworth, *Historical Collections*, 4 vols. (London, 1680–92), iv, 519).

[15] The legislation had been initially introduced in the form of an ordinary bill (December 7, 1641) but agreement of the House of Commons to a second reading was given only on December 31, 1641. See Simond D'Ewes, *The Journal of Simonds D'Ewes from the first Recess of the Long Parliament to the withdrawal of King Charles from London*, ed. William Havelock Coates (New Haven, Conn., 1942), pp. 248, 372. According to Clarendon, the act, considered as a bill, was passed by the House of Commons on January 20, 1642 and then accepted by the House of Lords under a threat of force. Passage in the form of an ordinance came on February 14, 1642. See Edward, Earl of Clarendon, *The History of the Rebellion and Civil Wars in England*, 6 vols. (Oxford, 1888), i, 522, 551–2, 570.

[16] Cobbett, vol. ii, col. 1114.   [17] *Ibid*. col. 1152.   [18] *Ibid*. col. 1207.

eligerit.'[19] On Parliament's construction of this language, he was therefore bound to approve any statute which the people (through Parliament) might wish to have (reading *eligerit* to mean 'shall have chosen'). The very formula *le roi s'avisera*, by which the king traditionally signified his refusal to assent, was now adduced in proof that he must yield. It was a temporary suspension of assent rather than a flat denial, and it implied that where assent was repeatedly requested, or where the public need was urgent in Parliament's opinion, the king was bound to yield. In the last analysis, the 'negative voice,' or veto, of the king applied only to private bills, or to public bills affecting individuals such as pardons or grants of favors.[20]

In the revolutionary atmosphere of the Interregnum, the argument had serious appeal even for thoughtful moderates. But in the more cautious mood of 1642, its persuasive force was weak. In an almost immediate reply by Charles – which could well have been written for him by Edward Hyde, later the Earl of Clarendon – the entire case was readily exploded. The Answer begins by questioning whether the clause on which Parliament relied was standard in the English oath. Even conceding that it still applied, the term *eligerit* can also mean 'has chosen,' in the past. That this must be the better reading is surely indicated 'by the reference it hath to custom (*consuetudines*),' as also by the interpretation put on it 'by the perpetual practice of succeeding ages.'[21] But even waiving this most formidable objection, the king of England could hardly have intended to encompass an act like the Militia Ordinance as one of the possible proposals to which he must assent, since it took away the essence of his power to command, which Charles had called the 'flower of his crown.'[22] The king no doubt is bound, as Parliament had said, to remedy any 'mischiefs and damages which happened to his people.' But he is not bound to renounce his right of judgment as to what the remedy shall be. Finally,

---

[19] *Ibid.* col. 1303 (Rushworth, IV, 580).
[20] *Ibid.* col. 1304 (Rushworth, IV, 581).
[21] *Ibid.* cols. 1337–8 (Rushworth, IV, 593).
[22] *Ibid.* col. 1070.

the phrase *le roi s'avisera*, 'if it be no denial, is no consent.'[23]

In the other argument, which was far more persuasive at the time, the right of Parliament to make binding law without the king's consent was derived from its status as the highest court. Thus in a declaration of May 19, 1642 (to cite but one of many), Charles was reminded by the two houses of their earlier warning

> that if his majesty refused to join with us therein [i.e. the Militia Ordinance] the two houses of Parliament, being the supreme court and highest council of the kingdom, were enabled by their own authority to provide for the repulsing of such imminent and evident danger, not by any new law of their own making, as has been untruly suggested by your majesty, but by the most ancient law of this kingdom, even that which is fundamental to the constitution and subsistence of it.[24]

Parliament was undoubtedly the highest court of England. In that capacity it did not need the king's assent; and in judging controversies the two houses, or at least the Lords, were incidentally required to construe the meaning of the law authoritatively. But the Militia Ordinance was not an act of judicature, or interpretation of the law. It was obviously an act of legislation, or laying down of law. This is even suggested in the passage quoted, when the capacity of Parliament as the highest court is smoothly linked to its status as the 'highest council of the kingdom.' But in this latter capacity, as the royalists quickly pointed out, the king's express consent was needed for a binding act. Writing somewhat later, Bishop Sanderson was especially lucid in expressing this objection:

> The judges of other courts, forasmuch as their power is but ministerial and merely judicial, are bounded by the present laws and limited also by their own acts, so as they may neither swerve from the laws in giving judgment nor reverse their own judgments after they are given. But the high court of Parliament having (by reason of the king's supreme power residing therein) a power legislative as well as judicial are not so limited by any earthly power but that they may change and over-rule the laws and their own acts and pleasure. The king's personal assent therefore is

23 *Ibid*. col. 1338 (Rushworth, IV, 595).
24 *Ibid*. col. 1251.

14

not needful in those other courts which are bounded by those laws whereunto the king hath already given his personal assent. But unto any act of power beside, beyond, above or against the laws already established, we have been informed, and it seems to us very agreeable to reason, that the king's personal assent should be absolutely necessary, forasmuch as every such act is the exercise of a legislative rather than a judicial power; and no act of legislative in any community (by consent of all nations) can be valid unless it be confirmed by such person or persons as the sovereignty of the community resideth in. . .[25]

But the claim of power by the Parliament is even more remarkable. The fundamental law that it professes to 'declare' by passing ordinances is nothing less than the rule of *salus rei publicae* – the fundamental law of nature that the public shall be saved from harm. The two houses are accordingly entitled of their own initiative to find that an emergency exists and, without the king, to enact all measures that seem in their judgment to be needed. The power thus asserted extends to every right of sovereignty, and, carried to its logical conclusion, would encompass the power to depose as well. The right of the two houses to preserve the English people must necessarily take precedence over any other right or status established by the constitution. *Salus rei publicae* is 'fundamental to the constitution and subsistence' of the kingdom in the sense that it is antecedent to, and above, all other rules.

These larger implications are often left conveniently obscure. But from time to time they are more or less openly expressed. A particularly good example appears in the Answer to Charles of May 19, 1642:

[I]n this case of extreme danger, and his majesty's refusal, the ordinance of Parliament agreed upon by both houses for the militia, doth oblige the people and ought to be obeyed, by the fundamental laws of this kingdom. By all. . .[of the preceding] it doth appear that there is no color of this tax [by Charles] 'that we go about to introduce a new law,' much less

[25] Robert Sanderson, *Reasons of the Present Judgment of the University of Oxford Concerning the Solemn League and Covenant, the Negative Oath, the Ordinance Concerning Discipline* (1647), in *A Preservative against Schism and Rebellion. . .or A Resolution of the Most Important Cases of Conscience Relating to Government Both in Church and State*, 3 vols. (London, 1722), I, 354–6.

to exercise an arbitrary power, but indeed to prevent it. For this law is as old as the kingdom – that the kingdom must not be without a means to preserve itself; which, that it may be done without confusion, this nation hath entrusted certain hands with a power to provide in an ordinary and regular way for the good and safety of the whole; which power, by the constitution of this kingdom is in his majesty and his Parliament together. Yet since the prince, being but one person is more subject to accidents of nature and chance, whereby the commonwealth may be deprived of the fruit of that trust which was in part reposed in him; in cases of such necessity, that the kingdom may not be enforced presently to return to its first principles, and every man left to do what is right in his own eyes, without either guide or rule, the wisdom of this state hath entrusted the houses of Parliament to supply what shall be wanting on the part of the prince; as is evident by the constant custom and practice thereof in cases of nonage, natural disability, and captivity; and the like reason doth, and must, hold for the exercise of the same power in such cases where the royal trust cannot be or is not discharged, and that the kingdom runs an evident and imminent danger thereby; which danger, having been declared by the Lords and Commons in Parliament, there needs not the authority of any person or court to affirm, nor is it in the power of any person or court to revoke that judgment.[26]

Such arguments were so general, and fundamental, as it were, that they were hardly subject to objection on specifics. The best that Charles could do was to point out caustically that the idea of a trust to override his trust was to negate the entire monarchical component of the English constitution which he was now affecting to defend.

But [my] trust. . . [they] say ought to be managed by their advice, and the kingdom hath trusted them for that purpose – impossible! that the same trust should be irrevocably committed to us and our heirs forever and the same trust, and power beyond that trust (for such is the power they pretend) be committed to others. Did not the people that sent them look upon them as a body but temporary, and dissoluble at our pleasure; and can it be believed that they intended them for our guardians and controllers in the managing of that trust that God and the law hath granted to us and our posterity forever?[27]

Parliament's reply to all such charges is that it had not impaired the royal trust nor even claimed a right to do so. This is

---

[26] Cobbett, vol. II, col. 1262 (Clarendon, II, 99–100).
[27] *Ibid*. col. 1334 (Rushworth, IV, 591).

the point where the inconsistency in its position becomes evident. The extraordinary trust it had asserted clearly indicates a right of deposition, and at the very least a power (and a duty) to suspend the office of the king until the emergency was over. In the passage quoted, the latter power is mentioned almost in so many words when the two houses refer to temporary disqualification of a king for nonage or other disability. Yet for all of this, Parliament, strenuously attempting to avoid that claim, maintained that Charles' powers were untouchable and that none of them had been impaired by anything that Parliament had done. The king at all times was legally or virtually present in Parliament, no matter where he was in person. He consented to all enactments of the two houses by his royal, legal will, his personal refusals notwithstanding. The subject, therefore, was obligated to take the orders of the two houses as if they were the king's commands. Parliament, as in the Militia Ordinance, merely 'signified' his will unto the subject. The legal subterfuge, accordingly, was a separation of the king's official from his personal capacities.[28]

In justification of this procedure, Parliament claimed that it was a familiar principle of English law. In every lower court, verdicts were rendered as the king's judgment even though the king was absent; the judgment was still considered his even when the verdict went against him in the persons of his officers. The same principle, Parliament contended, must apply to the highest court as well, 'the judgment whereof is, in the eye of the law the king's judgment in his highest court, though the king in his person be neither present nor consenting thereto.'[29] And this, inevitably, applies to acts of the two Houses in all capacities of Parliament.

The high court of Parliament is not only a court of judicature. . .but it is likewise a council to provide for the necessity, to prevent the imminent dangers, and preserve the public peace and safety of the kingdom, and to declare the king's pleasure in those things that are requisite thereunto; and what they do herein hath the stamp of royal authority, although

[28] See above, p. 11.
[29] Cobbett, vol. ii, col. 1261 (Clarendon, ii, 99).

his majesty, seduced by evil counsel, do, in his own person, oppose or interrupt the same; for the king's supreme power and royal pleasure is exercised and declared in the high court of law and council after a more eminent and obligatory manner than it can be by any personal act or resolution of his own.

Hence even if a command of the two houses should be 'against the king's will and personal command, yet they are the king's judgments' and binding on every court and subject in the realm.[30]

The flaw in this analogy is that judges of inferior courts decide by rules of law which the king has precedently approved. Only thus can his consent to the verdict be presumed. But it cannot be presumed when the high court of Parliament, acting in its legislative capacity, undertakes to alter law. Inferior judges, furthermore, were technically ministers appointed by the king, whereas the two houses were constituted independently. Hence even for judicial business, the king's consent to proceedings in Parliament had to be signified by the presence of his seal, which was no longer in Parliament's possession after May 21, 1642.[31] The difficulties, once again, are put most elegantly by Sanderson:

The judges in inferior courts. . .are to all act in his [the king's] name and by his authority. . .sitting there not by any proper interest of their own but only in right of the king, whose judges they are, and therefore they are called the king's judges and his ministers. But in the high court of Parliament, the Lords and Commons sit there in council with the king as supreme judge for the good of the whole realm; and therefore they are not called the king's judges but the king's council. And they have their several proper rights and interests peculiar and distinct both between themselves and from that of the kings – by reason whereof they become distinct orders or, as of late times they have been styled (in this sense we conceive) three distinct estates. Each of which being supposed to be the best conservators of their own proper interest, if the power of any one estate should be presumed to be virtually present in the other two, that estate must needs be inevitably liable to suffer in the proper

[30] *Ibid.* col. 1357 (Rushworth, IV, 551–2).
[31] After much hesitation, Lord Keeper Littleton had smuggled it off to the king at York.

interests thereof; which might quickly prove destructive to the whole kingdom, the safety and prosperity of the whole consisting in the conservation of the just rights and proper interests of them in parts, viz: the king, lords, and commons inviolate and entire.[32]

More generally, the royalists protested that separation of a king's powers from his person denied his status as a king and in this they were undoubtedly correct. If the prince's legal, or royal, will is determined by the votes of Parliament, then all his powers must be vested in that body. As Samuel Eaton, a republican, would later put it, 'This distinction between the man and the king is but a notional conceit; for take away the man, and where then is the king?'[33]

Nevertheless, the line of reasoning pursued by Parliament had only to be carried one step further to yield a right of war against Charles' government without appearing to suspend his office or to remove his sacrosanctity. In January 1642, the two houses decided to assume control of the important magazine at Hull in order to forestall its seizure by the king. John Hotham, a member of the House of Commons, was accordingly commissioned to gather certain trained bands in the area and to establish a garrison within the town. The instructions given Hotham already contained the legal formula that rendered him accountable to the two houses alone. He was forbidden to 'deliver up the town of Hull, or the magazine there, or any part thereof without the king's authority signified unto him by the Lords and Commons assembled in the Parliament.'[34]

After many protests and a number of minor military probes designed to test the determination of the two houses (and of Hotham), Charles decided on dramatic confrontation. He appeared in person with a retinue of guards and demanded to 'enter the town and to inspect and make use of his magazine.' Hotham denying him admittance, Charles solemnly declared

---

[32] Sanderson, *Reasons*, in *A Preservative*, I, 352–4.
[33] Samuel Eaton, *A Reply to an Answer Pretending to Refute Some Positions which tended to Make the Oath of Allegiance void and Non-obliging* (London, 1650), p. 25.
[34] Cobbett, vol. II, cols. 1028–9 (Rushworth, IV, 496).

that this refusal was an act of treason.[35] It was a threat of force, and in a sense the use of force, to constrain the person of the king.

Parliament, in defending Hotham, now made its clearest statement on the right of forcible resistance to the king. Far from defying the king, Hotham had acted 'in obedience to his majesty and his authority,' for a distinction must be drawn between Charles' royal and his personal will. '[L]evying war against his [the king's] laws and authority, though not against his person, is levying war against the king; but the levying of forces against his personal commands, though accompanied with his presence, and not against his laws and authority but in maintenance thereof, is no levying of war against the king but for him.'[36]

At this point, however, no good reason could be given why Charles should not have been deposed. Parliament continued to insist that the king could do no wrong. But the meaning of this rule in English law could not be stretched to cover Charles' behavior as Parliament officially described it. Under English procedure, illegal orders by the king were void. An officer of the king was not required or entitled to enforce them; if he sought to do so to the damage of a subject, he could be brought before the courts and sued, his plea of royal orders notwithstanding. In this sense, the wrong was his and not the king's. But the tacit assumption, which alone makes sense of this procedure, is that the king, authoritatively informed that his order was illegal, would desist from attempting to effect it. This precisely, according to the Parliament's account, is what Charles had flagrantly refused to do, and on so many points and in such a fashion as to prosecute a design to subvert the English constitution. Charles thereby had given up the immunity attaching to his office. If Parliament was right in saying that it had been entrusted by the people with overriding power to preserve public safety, it had not only a right but an obligation to depose. Once again the point is stated most incisively by Eaton:

[35] *Ibid*. col. 1187.   [36] *Ibid*. col. 1310 (Rushworth, IV, 585).

Now we know that the oath of allegiance was made to the king as king, and so the subject has nothing to do with him in point of obedience or allegiance save only as king; that is, when he rules according to the law. Again, the oath of allegiance being to a legal king, when the person of the king is a tyrant and breaks the law and overthrows all courts of justice, where is then this legal king? And if there be none, the subject is then discharged from his oath of allegiance.[37]

Parliament's position thus embraced a contradiction. By disclaiming power to depose, it implicitly conceded a sphere of power in the king which was independent of the Parliament and which Parliament was forbidden to assume. And yet it had assumed his powers. Conversely, by assuming all of Charles' powers, it had stripped him of his office and immunities – almost in so many words. Yet it continued to insist that he was sacrosanct. This was now to become a dilemma for its publicists. In the aftermath of 1642, Parliament itself abstained from further refinements of its doctrine, at least by way of official declarations. Wisely perhaps, in view of the problems we have mentioned, it simply cited its previous conclusions arrived at in the paper war. The entire burden of replying to royalist critiques had thus to be assumed by those who wrote on its behalf. They at least were required to provide a more extensive rationale. And it is in the writings of these publicists that the basic contradiction becomes fully evident.

[37] Eaton, *A Reply*, pp. 24-5.

2

The Parliamentary publicists

THE VARIOUS PUBLICISTS who wrote for Parliament in the early 1640s were bound to consider the issue of ultimate, constituent power in a mixed constitution. They may be divided into two main groups by the way they treat this question. One group of writers explicitly contended that constituent power of the people, as represented in a Parliament, is a necessary condition of all legitimate monarchies and especially of limited monarchies. This group could readily justify the vast powers asserted by the Parliament to protect the people's safety. But it could provide no reasoned principle by which the king was independent of the Parliament and why he could not be and had not been deposed. The writers in the other group, conversely, insisting upon royal sacrosanctity, denied constituent authority, either in the people or in Parliament. They could thus explain why the king was independent and could not be removed. But they could find no grounds as to why Parliament should be legally entitled to engage in resistance, even short of deposition.[1]

The earliest major pamphlet of the first variety is Henry Parker's *Observations upon Some of His Majesty's Late Answers and Expresses*, which appeared in 1642. As the title

[1] For other treatments of constitutionalist theories in this period, see J. W. Allen, *English Political Thought 1603–1644* (London, 1938); and Margaret Atwood Judson, *The Crisis of the Constitution* (New Brunswick, 1949), ch. IX. For the influence of French and other continental theories on English doctrines from the Elizabethan period to the Glorious Revolution, see J. H. M. Salmon, *The French Religious Wars in English Political Thought* (Oxford, 1959).

indicates, it is a reply by Parker to several manifestoes issued in the name of Charles, and it was most especially directed to an Answer of June 4, 1642, which was perhaps the most incisive statement up to that point of royalist objections to the legal claims of Parliament. Parker begins, significantly, not with the positive law of the English state but with the original act of constitution by which the kingship was said to have been created. Charles had contended that his royal authority came not only from the law, but was derived directly from the will of God. Parker answers that royal power is from God only in the sense that God corroborates the free decision of the people, from whose consent all legitimate authority derives. 'Power is originally inherent in the people and is nothing but that might and vigor which such and such a society of men contains in itself; and when by such and such a law of common consent and agreement it is devolved into such and such hands, God confirms that law. And man is the free and voluntary author, the law is the instrument, and God is the establisher of both.'[2]

From this premise certain conclusions are deduced which were well known in the monarchomach tradition. Since the king in his legal capacity is created by the people as a 'true efficient cause,' the people, as the cause, must be higher than that which is effect (*quicquid efficit tale est magis tale*). There is superiority in the king, but only with respect to the people taken severally, not to the people taken as a whole. Although *singulis major*, he is *universis minor*. All royal power is therefore subject to conditions.[3] In an interesting advance on the monarchomachs, Parker would apply this principle to monarchs who might be qualified as 'absolute' because their acts did not require the consent of a body independently constituted for that purpose. Such monarchs too, for Parker, are created by the people subject to the condition that they promote the public good.[4] But this was an early and inadequate arrangement.

[2] Henry Parker, *Observations upon Some of His Majesty's Late Answers and Expresses* (2nd ed. London, 1643), p. 1.
[3] *Ibid.* p. 2.
[4] *Ibid.* p. 4.

Among more civilized and experienced peoples, who have learned the dangers of monopolistic government, first laws, and then parliaments, were imposed upon the king in order to restrain him in the public's interest. Such was the sequence and the motives that produced the English constitution.[5]

Parker does not immediately insist that the representatives of the people, once assembled, are supreme in all respects, at least for ordinary purposes, for he felt obliged to take some account of royal independence. Charles, in several of his Answers, had chosen the mixture of the English constitution as a line of defense against the Parliament. There were legal claims by Parliament, said Charles, which he could not acknowledge as legitimate, as well as proposals for a settlement to which he could not give assent, because the English constitution was composed of three independent estates of which the king was intended to be one. Charles, accordingly, could not compromise his independence without violation of his oath of office and his sacred obligation to defend the constitution. Indeed, if Charles should yield on this, all other law would be in jeopardy, including the security of property. He would be countenancing the erection of an unchecked and therefore arbitrary power in the two houses, whose unlawful tendencies were already manifest by their effort to deprive Charles of much that belonged to him as king. The most celebrated statement, although not perhaps the best juridically,[6] was his *Answer to the Nineteen Propositions* (of Parliament) of June 18, 1642.

There being three kinds of government among men, absolute monarchy, aristocracy, and democracy; and all these having their particular conveniences and inconveniences; the experience and wisdom of your ancestors, hath so molded this out of a mixture of these, as to give to this kingdom (as far as humane prudence can provide) the conveniences

---

[5] *Ibid.* pp. 14–16. A similar thought also is found in the *Vindiciae contra tyrannos*. See Julian H. Franklin, *Constitutionalism and Resistance in the Sixteenth Century* (New York, 1969), p. 169.

[6] Charles, ill-advised, represents the kingship as but one of three estates, thus casting doubt on its supremacy. But the view he took was sometimes suggested in the legal tradition. See below p. 25, n. 9.

of all three, without the inconveniences of any one, as long as the balance hangs even between the three estates, and they run jointly on in their proper channel (begetting vertue and fertility in the meadows on both sides), and the overflowing of either on either side, raise no deluge or inundation.[7]

Charles' defense was so deeply rooted in English law and practice that it could not simply be ignored.[8] Rather than dispute the mixture of the English constitution, Parker cheerfully accepts it. He admits that legislative power is divided between 'king and kingdom' and that ordinarily neither one can act without the other. The right to act alone is thus restricted to extraordinary circumstances; even then a certain symmetry is at least hypothetically envisaged. Parker admits at one point that not only may the people act without the king in an emergency in order to secure their safety, but the king might conceivably act alone to save the kingdom where the people are 'unnaturally' misled.[9]

The question now presented, however, is who shall be the final judge in a dispute between king and kingdom and in one quick step Parker goes back upon the principle of mixture by locating that finality in Parliament. The main argument is the reflection – partly prudential and partly juridical – that in the very last analysis sovereignty cannot be divided. In every state, he erroneously assumes, there has to be a final power *within*

[7] John Rushworth, *Historical Collections*, IV (London, 1692), 731. The character, authorship, and influence of this Answer by Charles is considered at length in Corinne Comstock Weston, *English Constitutional Theory and the House of Lords 1596–1832*. See especially pp. 24ff. (New York, 1970).
[8] The idea of the king as an independent 'estate' of Parliament can be found among major legal commentators of the sixteenth and seventeenth centuries. One example is Henry Finch, *Nomotechnia* (London, 1613), 'The assembly of these three estates, i.e. the king, nobility, and commons which make up the body of the realm, is called a Parliament and their decree an act of Parliament, for without all three...there is no act of Parliament.' Neither Parliament nor any of its publicists were willing to abandon this idea completely no matter how much they might try to weaken its force. (For the contrasting continental attitude, see above pp. 4–5.) And most Parliamentary writers are willing to concede a 'negative voice,' at least in some circumstances.
[9] Parker, *Observations*, p. 16.

the constitution, and there is no safer or wiser repository for that power than a body of the people's representatives:

> That there is an arbitrary power somewhere, 'tis true, 'tis necessary, and no inconvenience follows upon it; every man has an absolute power over himself, but because no man can hurt himself, this power is not dangerous, nor need to be restrained. So every state has an arbitrary power over itself, and there is no danger in it for the same reason. If the state entrusts this to one man, or a few, there may be danger in it; but the Parliament is neither one nor a few; it is indeed the state itself.[10]

In this decisive passage the overriding right of Parliament is not explicitly derived from the constituent power of the general community. But Parker's phrase 'the state itself' implicitly equates the two; and in other passages the identification is expressed. Although the king, no less than Parliament, derives his power from the people, the power derived is more 'eminent' in Parliament because the 'essence of the people' is contained in it. When the people decided to put restraints upon the king, public assemblies were instituted in which 'the whole community in its underived majesty shall convene to do justice... and that the vastness of its own bulk may not breed confusion, by virtue of election and representation a few shall act for many, the wise shall consent for the few, the virtue of all shall redound to some, and the prudence of some shall redound to all.'[11]

However derived, the ultimate and arbitrary power of Parliament is inconsistent with independent power in the king. As might be expected, Parker cites and endorses all the subterfuges by which Parliament assumed the royal power, and he reproduces the familiar arguments to justify them. At one point, indeed, he imports an analogy which seems remarkable by modern notions. Speaking of the duty of the king to yield

[10] *Ibid.* p. 21. On the emergence, with such views, of the idea of Parliamentary supremacy in England, see Margaret Atwood Judson, 'Henry Parker and the Theory of Parliamentary Sovereignty,' in *Essays in History and Political Theory in Honor of Charles Howard McIlwain* (Cambridge, Mass., 1936), pp. 138–67; and J. R. Pole, *The Seventeenth Century: The Sources of Legislative Power* (Charlottesville, 1969), pp. 10ff.

[11] *Observations*, p. 15.

consent to Parliament's deliberate requests, he cites the Venetian constitution as the model of a proper monarchy[12] – which is, we may note, a favorite theme in the monarchomach tradition.

But Parker, after all of this, cannot explain why Parliament should not be authorized to diminish the powers of the king-ship, even for ordinary purposes, and to remove an occupant from office – which is the official position that he felt obliged to rationalize. On the first point, the best he can offer is an assurance to the royalists that no proper English Parliament would ever think of doing such a thing. Replying to the plea of Charles that to concede the demands of the two houses would open up a path to tyranny, Parker protests that 'no age will furnish us one example of any parliament freely elected and held that ever did injure a whole kingdom, or exercise a tyranny, nor is there any possibility it should. The king may safely leave his highest rights to Parliament, for none knows better, or affects more, the sweetness of this so well-balanced a monarchy than they do, and it hath been often in their power under great provocation to load that rule with follies – but they would not.'[13] This quite obviously is a political prophecy rather than a legal principle.

On the second issue, the right of deposition, there is no more than a passing mention, coming almost at the very end, that the king can do no wrong. Although ministers of the king may be held responsible for his illegal acts, the king himself may not. 'The king as to his own person is not to be forcibly repelled in ill-doing, nor is he accountable for ill done. Law has only a

---

[12] The basic point is that princes should not prefer their own wills to the considered will of the realm: 'I will enlarge myself no longer upon this endless theme. Let us look upon the Venetians and such other free nations. Why are they so extremely zealous over their princes...? It is merely for fear of this bondage: that their princes will dote upon their own wills, and despise public councils and laws in respect of their own private opinions. Were not this the sting of monarchy, of all forms it...[would be] the most exquisite; and to all nations it would be the most desirable. Happy are those monarchs who qualify this sting, and happy are those peoples which are governed by such monarchs' (*ibid*. p. 26).

[13] *Ibid*. p. 22.

directive, not a coactive, force upon his person.'[14] Given all that Parker has already said on the people's constituent authority, no rationale for this is possible, and none is offered. The maxim is simply stated as a brute fact of English law.

Another example of this lack of consequence – even more glaring because the theory is otherwise so lucid – is Charles Herle's *A Fuller Answer...*, which appeared somewhat later in 1642. *A Fuller Answer* is one of several replies by Herle in his exchange with Henry Ferne, who was the most redoubtable polemicist for non-resistance in the early 1640s. Ferne contended that the king of England, although limited, was nonetheless a superior authority above all others, and that all resistance, even to unjust commands (if any) was thus forbidden by the law of God.[15] But in the English constitution, Herle replies, the two houses are independent and coordinate authorities. In their collective capacities, and when assembled, their members are the king's partners rather than his subjects. The two houses were therefore justified in assuming royal powers temporarily when Charles defaulted on his trust. In any joint enterprise, one partner may supply the defect of the other:

Before we judge of what Parliament can do in England, it will be needful to know what kind of government this of England's is. We are therefore to know that England's is not a simply subordinative and absolute, but a coordinative and mixed monarchy. This mixture or co-ordination is in the very supremacy of power itself; otherwise the monarchy were not mixed. All monarchies have a mixture of subordinate and other officers in them, but here the monarchy, or highest power, is itself compounded of three coordinate estates, a king and two houses of Parliament. Unto this mixed power, no subordinate authority may in any case make resistance. The rule holds still: *subordinata non pugnant*, subordinates may not strive. But in this our mixed highest power there is no subordination, but a coordination, and here the other rule holds as true: *coordinata invicem supplent*, coordinates supply each other.[16]

[14] *Ibid.* p. 44.
[15] For a more elaborate statement of Ferne's position, see below pp. 34ff.
[16] Charles Herle, *A Fuller Answer to a Treatise Written by Dr. Ferne* (London, 1642), p. 3.

Parliament, accordingly, was simply acting to discharge its trust: 'So then the government, by law its rule unto safety its end, is ordinarily betrusted to the king, wherein if he fails to follow the rule, law, or to its end, safety, his coordinates in this mixture of the supreme power must according to their trusts supply.'[17]

The question now arises as to why it is the Parliament rather than the king which is the final judge as to whether a default has taken place. Herle, like Parker, speaks of the need for final arbitrament in any constitution, which is best reposed in a representative assembly.[18] But the prudential element now becomes unmistakably subsidiary to an argument from constituent authority.

In Herle's account the king – and Parliament as well – is bound by fundamental law, the most sacred article of which is the rule of *salus populi*. But all fundamental law was originally constituted by an act of the people's representative, which is thus entitled to construe its meaning and declare what it requires when it judges as the 'highest court.' The king, on the other hand, cannot have this highest power since the office and duties of the kingship were themselves created by the two houses, or by some earlier version of that body. And since the two houses form a corporation, which does not lose its character and power when its members change, their original power to preserve the people must lie within them still.

Now as this mixture, the mean unto the fuller safety, dies not – 'tis not personal but incorporate and corporations (the law says) die not – so that reason or wisdom of state that first contrived it dies not either. It lives still in that which the law calls the reason of this kingdom, the votes and ordinances of the Parliament, which being the same (in the construction of the law) with that which first contrived the government must needs have still power to apply this coordination to its end, safety, as well it had first to introduce it; otherwise it [the government] should not still continue in the office of a mean to its end.[19]

As this passage clearly indicates, Herle does not contemplate the use of this authority by Parliament to alter the office of the

[17] *Ibid.* p. 8.   [18] *Ibid.* p. 14.   [19] *Ibid.* p. 8.

kingship or to remove a tyrannical incumbent. It is presented as a power to preserve the constitution, not to alter it; as if the only proper means in an emergency is to assume the functions of the king on a temporary basis. But there is not a single word in Herle to justify these limitations. It is as though he senses the difficulty and can find no way to overcome it. For the power to preserve the people must surely include the power to change the way that it is governed and most certainly the right of deposition.

We may presume, however, that Herle, like Parker, sincerely believed that there would never be a need for radical solutions, and that no proper English Parliament would ever contemplate such measures. The common people, to be sure, might engage in revolution if they were entitled to act without the Parliament, which was a standard royalist objection. But Herle replies that he never intended to accord the people such a right, and that none is implied by anything he said.

A second question begged [by Ferne] is that in case the king and Parliament should neither discharge their trusts, the people might rise and make resistance against them both, a position which no man I know maintains. The Parliament is the people's own consent, which once passed they cannot revoke. He [Ferne] still pursues his own dread of the people's resuming power, whereas we acknowledge no power can be employed but what is reserved and the people have reserved no power in themselves from themselves in Parliament.[20]

20 *Ibid.* p. 25. The right of deposition in the people is generally denied by English Parliamentary publicists of this period – whether expressly as in Herle or by clear implication as in Parker. The one exception among well-known writers in the early 1640s is the Scottish publicist, Samuel Rutherford, who is avowedly following his fellow Scot of the previous century, Buchanan. See *Lex, Rex* (London, 1644), Preface. But Rutherford, we should note, does not use this idea to clarify the concept of mixed monarchy. He assumes that Parliament may substitute fully for the people, and is the source, or 'fountain,' of the king's authority. His view of the relationship of king and Parliament in a mixed constitution is thus very similar to Herle's: 'The Parliament is thus coordinate ordinarily with the king in the power of making laws. But the coordination in the king's part is by derivation; in the Parliament's part *originaliter* and *formaliter* as in the fountain. In ordinary there is a coordination, but if the king turn tyrant, the Estates are to use their fountain-power' (*ibid.* p. 210). We should perhaps also note here that Parker would later change his

It is worth pointing out perhaps that this restriction on the people vis-à-vis the Parliament imports no similar restriction on the Parliament vis-à-vis the king. On the contrary, the fullness of the people's concession to the Parliament removes the only principle on which the latter's power to depose could be restricted. For Herle, indeed, its constituent authority is not only admitted to be arbitrary, but is particularly described as such even though he does not draw the final inference.

[A]s the government, in the form and qualification of it, was at first an act of the will and arbitrary, so, it still remaining the same, it must remain somewhere arbitrary still, else our forefathers should not convey that same government to us which they began; they cannot bind us in that wherein they were themselves free. . .It is the privilege of God's law only to bind arbitrarily. Nowhere should the arbitrariness of this faculty reside but where it was at first in the consent and reason of the state, which, as we have seen, the law places in the votes of Parliament.[21]

The last work to be considered in this group is William Prynne's voluminous treatise on *The Sovereign Power of Parliaments and Kingdoms*, which was published in installments beginning in 1643. It is with this work that the inconsistency in Herle and Parker at last becomes overt.

Prynne, to begin with, takes the same position as the others on the constituent authority of Parliament. Widely read in monarchomach sources, he liberally cites their arguments and often reproduces them at length. All legitimate kings are instituted by the people subject to conditions, and the power of the people is equated with the power of the two houses of Parliament. But Prynne is even more insistent than the others on the supremacy of Parliament even in ordinary circumstances – in large measure because he is thoroughly persuaded that

position on individual resistance when he came to support the Commonwealth. Since the act by which the government was altered came from outside the Parliament, he felt bound to say that 'extreme, eminent, and otherwise insuperable dangers give private persons, yea single private persons, an extraordinary warrant to defend themselves and others. . .' (*Scotland's Holy War. . .as also an Answer to a paper entitled Some Considerations in relation to. . .the Engagement* (London, 1651), p. 25).
[21] *Fuller Answer*, p. 17.

there is no royal veto for important public bills. The consequence of supremacy is pressed so relentlessly by Prynne that the kingship is all but completely dissolved in the Parliament of which it is a part: 'King, Lords, and Commons by the common law make but one entire corporation, and since then even in Parliament itself the major part oversways the rest, yea the king himself (who hath no absolute negative voice...), doubtless the whole, or major part of the Parliament (which in law is the whole) is above the king, the chief member of it.'[22] Since the king, moreover, is assumed to be always present in a Parliament, the power of the two houses to carry on affairs without him is complete.

But of greater interest for present purposes are a number of passing comments made by Prynne on Parliament's constituent authority. Seeking to show how exalted are its powers, he cites the fate of Edward II and Richard II as proof of its power to depose. Parliament, and the other writers we have mentioned, had tactfully abstained from the slightest mention of these cases. But Prynne introduces them as 'sleeping precedents' to warn the king.[23] And speaking of the existing situation, he seems at one point to discard the maxim that the king can do no wrong. Technically at least, the king may become a 'traitor to the realm' and 'forfeit his very right and title to the crown.'[24]

Yet for all of this, the thought of deposing Charles I seemed impious to Prynne. Against the charge by Ferne and other royalists that Parliament had levied war against the king, he indignantly replies that it had 'renounced any such disloyal intention or design at all.'[25] The war was waged against an army of malignants, as Parliament had said, and not against the person of the king or his 'just supremacy and prerogatives royal.'[26]

With the inconsistent overtones removed, Prynne's position, very likely, is that deposition is not so much forbidden as

---

[22] William Prynne, *The Sovereign Power of Parliaments and Kingdoms* (London, 1643), Part I, p. 42.
[23] *Ibid*. Part I, p. 86.   [24] *Ibid*. Part III, p. 7.
[25] *Ibid*. Part III, p. 62.   [26] *Ibid*. Part I, p. 103.

renounced. The right perhaps existed, but Parliament had 'loyally' decided not to exercise it. Here the difficulty enters. If Parliament possessed the power to depose, it was bound to use it against Charles by its obligation to protect the people's safety. His continuation on the throne was of manifest help to the 'malignant party,' and he could not be exculpated personally. Since Charles had not only been deceived, but had also been 'seduced' by wicked counsellors, it was the duty of Parliament, on Prynne's conception of its powers, to declare that Charles had forfeited his crown.

Hence in each of these three publicists, resistance is legitimated at the cost of failing to account for the independence of the king in the English constitution. Indeed they emphasize Parliamentary supremacy so much, that one might be tempted to see them as covert republicans. Yet this is not the mood of what they say in the early 1640s, nor is it a clue to their subsequent behavior. Although Parker supported the Commonwealth in the aftermath of 1649, Herle abstained, and Prynne was bitterly, even fanatically, opposed. Prynne, the legalist, had many technical objections to the Rump. But the dominant motif is his loyalty to the good old constitution in which King, Lords, and Commons were in balance.[27] Hence in the absence of clear evidence to the contrary, it is safer to assume that all publicists in the early 1640s were still attached to the existing constitution, and that the three whom we have just considered were pushed toward Parliamentary supremacy by a real theoretical dilemma. They could find no other basis to legitimate resistance.

The second group of publicists includes William Bridge, Jeremiah Burroughs, and Philip Hunton, among whom the last is so much more sophisticated that we shall consider him separately, treating the other two together. All three writers literally believed that the king's authority derived from God. They thus confronted the Parliamentary dilemma, as it were, from the other side. For on their assumption of the prince's

[27] Among other statements is his *Summary Reasons Against the New Oath and Engagement* (London, 1649), in which see especially p. 4.

33

sacrosanctity, deposition was excluded and resistance difficult to justify.

There was, of course, a more liberal interpretation of authority derived from God that was well-known in European thought. In the monarchomach tradition, which is followed by Prynne and Parker among other Englishmen, the king's authority derives from God by mediation of the people, which is thus entitled to enforce restrictions on the ruler's power. But the more literal construction, in which power came from God directly, was still powerful in European thought. It seemed to be confirmed in England by the law of treason, the oath of allegiance, and also by the oath of supremacy, which avowed the king to be the supreme head of the English church. There was, however, a constitutional consideration also. Authorization through the people as the monarchomachs and the preceding group of publicists conceived, was tied to Parliamentary supremacy. But Burroughs, Bridge, and Hunton were persuaded that the king of England was in some sense or another supreme within the constitution and independent of the Parliament. Hence by political conviction as well as by religious scruple, they could not admit constituent authority in any human agent. They were bound to hold that the king of England received authority from God directly, and that this sacrosanctity was not merely a brute fact of English law but a fundamental principle of government.

The problem for these writers, then, was how to avoid the absolutist implications with which this conception of authority was traditionally associated. A line of reasoning that seemed to point to a solution had already been suggested, ironically enough, by their arch-antagonist, Henry Ferne. Attempting to show that resistance to Charles I was sinful, Ferne inevitably insisted that his authority derived from God directly. But attempting also to account for the facts of the English constitution, Ferne concluded that God conferred qualified authority where a people, free to do so, expressed a wish for limitations. Absolute monarchy was, to be sure, *exemplo divino*. It was the form of government which God commended and which he had conferred on Adam as a patriarch. But absolute monarchy was not on that account *jure divino* or *jure naturae*. It was not the form of government on which God insisted either by express command or by the law of nature. Where, then, a people became free, for one reason or another, of obligations to an antecedent absolute authority, it was permitted by the law of God to choose that form of government it thought was best.[28] This is one way in which limited kingship may arise. Another is when a king, originally absolute, voluntarily limits his power by a promise – which Hunton would call an act of 'after-condescent grace.'[29]

But Ferne will not concede that these arrangements entail constituent authority in human agents. 'The power of government itself is of God, however the person be designed [i.e. designated] or that power qualified according to the several forms of government by these laws that are established, or those grants that are procured for the people's security.'[30] Pure governance – in other words, the simple right to wield coercive power – derives from God directly. But it is conveyed by God according to the arrangements as to form and mode of succession that the human agents, free to do so, have adopted. 'The power itself, or that sufficiency of authority to govern which is in monarchy or aristocracy, abstractly considered [apart] from the qualification of either form, is an efflux or constitution subordinate to that providence, an ordinance of that *Dixi*, that silent word by which the world was first made and is still governed by God.'[31]

Even a limited king, then, is accountable to God alone for the use of his coercive power, and that power, which the people has not constituted, it can never be entitled to resume. This is not to say, however, that all kings are immune to deposition.

[28] Henry Ferne, *Conscience Satisfied*...(Oxford, 1643), pp. 8–9. This work is in answer to several replies to his first treatise, *The Resolving of Conscience* (Cambridge, 1642).
[29] *Resolving*, p. 21. *Conscience Satisfied*, pp. 12, 33. Ferne adopts Hunton's term in *A Reply to Several Treatises*...(Oxford, 1643), pp. 15–17.
[30] *Resolving*, p. 18.
[31] *Ibid*. p. 17.

Where the consent of a people to a kingship is contractual in form, its obligation to obey is conditioned on the king's performance. The people would then have requested and received from God an ultimate power in itself. But Ferne insists, dogmatically, that the existence of a contract cannot be inferred from every intervention of consent. The contract has to be explicit. The only sure sign that it exists is an oath of coronation in which the king expressly acknowledges a right in the people to withdraw allegiance if he fails to fulfill his obligations. But this applies only to certain elective kingships like the Swedish and the Polish, which are not perhaps true monarchies at all, and surely not to England.[32] Indeed, to remove all doubt about the English case, Ferne insists that the original institution of the existing line of kings goes back to conquest, not consent.[33] There is thus no suggestion of a contract. The limitations included in the English constitution arose from acts of after-condescent grace.[34]

[32] The basic point is that since absolute monarchy is original and recommended by the law of God, there is a presumption against the right of a people to resume a king's power unless it is expressly stipulated. 'The words "capitulation" or "covenant" are now much used to make men believe the king's admittance to the crown is altogether conditional, as in the merely elective kingdoms of Poland and Sweden, etc., whereas our king is king before he comes to the coronation, which is sooner or later at his pleasure, but is always to be in due time in regard of that security his people receive by his taking the oath and he again mutually from them, in which performance there is something like a covenant – all but the forfeiture. The king there promises and binds himself by oath to performance. Could they in this covenant show us an agreement between the king and his people, that in case he will not discharge his trust, then it shall be lawful for the estates of the kingdom by arms to resist and provide for the safety thereof, it would be something' (*ibid.* p. 21).

[33] Ferne would concede that the earliest kingship was elective. But that arrangement was superseded by subsequent conquests. *Resolving*, p. 19; *Conscience Satisfied*, pp. 32–3.

[34] *Conscience Satisfied*, p. 33. Ferne has thus avoided the embarrassment of simple patriarchalism. Absolute patriarchal rule may be modified by agreement. He has also avoided the embarrassment of saying, with James I, that all public privileges in England depend simply on the ruler's grace. Although they may originate by after-condescent grace, they are concessions binding on the prince. Yet even so resistance is excluded in the absence of express reservations to the contrary. Ferne thus comes closer than any

Bridge and Burroughs do not reproduce this entire line of reasoning on the origins of royal power. They simply agree with Ferne that even a ruler who is subject to legal limitations may be accountable to God alone. They then attempt to push his conclusion one step further. Ferne contends that resistance as well as deposition in a kingship like the English is forbidden by the law of God. He concedes that private acts of self-defense are licit (which Bridge and Burroughs, incidentally, do not). But these are properly confined to the defense of one's self and one's immediate family against actual unjust violence. They do not extend to protection of the public's rights. All such larger acts, since they oppose the public power of the king, are violations of the ordinance of God.[35]

Bridge and Burroughs, on the other hand, assume an original right in the people to preserve itself, which is necessarily reserved when it freely consents to royal governance. That power, furthermore, may be exercised in its behalf by Parliament without violation of the English constitution. The two houses are somewhat independent, since they are 'officers of the kingdom, not only of the king.'[36] The two houses, furthermore, are entitled to use force since they empower sergeants-at-arms upon their own authority, and may appoint as many as are needed to prosecute their just commands.[37] Hence when tyranny is imminent, it is the right of Parliament to raise an army in order to defend the public.

As Bridge and Burroughs understand it, this procedure is compatible with royal sacrosanctity if two conditions are observed. Resistance, first of all, must stop short of deposition or alteration of the prince's power. In this sense the resort to arms is simply defensive. The second condition is that force

writer of the time to a theory of non-resistance compatible with a limited kingship. This is not to say, however, that it works. See below pp. 39–40. See also Robert Sheringham, *The King's Supremacy Asserted* (1660), which generally follows Ferne.

[35] *Resolving*, p. 7.
[36] William Bridge, *The Wounded Conscience Cured*...(London, 1642), pp. 4–5.
[37] *Ibid*. p. 6.

must not be deliberately used against the person of the king himself. It may be legitimately exercised only against his officers and instruments, who give force to his tyrannical designs. In this, says Bridge, neither 'do they [the people] so resume the power as to take away anything they gave the king, but so as to actuate the power [of self-preservation] which they always had left in themselves.'[38] Indeed, properly viewed, resort to arms in self-defense is not resistance to 'the power' in any sense at all. As Burroughs would have it, it is not even 'resisting abused power, for it is resisting no power at all. Abused power is the ill use of that which is given to men, but the ill use of what was never given to them more than to any other is abuse of their wills, but not abuse of their power. By power, I do not mean strength but authority.'[39]

There are, however, fundamental inconsistencies in this solution. The right of collective self-defense is an overriding public power, and when it is vested in a constituted body like the Parliament it describes a sovereign within the constitution. That status is already implied by the inherent right of Parliament to pass authoritative judgment on the conduct of the king. When Parliament initiates resistance, Bridge remarks, all subjects are obligated to obey its call.[40] But the sovereignty of Parliament is even more clearly implied by its right to raise an army and conduct a civil war. The act itself is an assumption, temporarily at least, of all political authority. And the very purpose of the war is, temporarily at least, to prevent the king from governing in any fashion whatsoever by depriving him of all his instruments. This, as Ferne objects, is clearly to resist 'the power.'[41] And it is indeed, as Dudley Digges insists, a complete assumption of the king's executive authority.[42]

[38] *Ibid.* p. 26.
[39] Jeremiah Burroughs, *A Brief Answer to Dr. Ferne's Book*...(London, 1643), pp. 7–8.
[40] *Wounded Conscience*, p. 3.
[41] Ferne, *Conscience Satisfied*, pp. 63–4.
[42] Dudley Digges, *The Unlawfulness of Subjects Taking up Arms against their Sovereign*, published 1643 (London, 1647), pp. 66–7, refutes Bridge's argument that if a court can send one agent to carry out its orders, it may

These difficulties are fairly obvious in Bridge and Burroughs, who contend with Ferne primarily on texts and examples drawn from Scripture and pay but slight attention to the legal issues. Philip Hunton, on the other hand, a theologian with extraordinary talent as a legal thinker, understood the legal problem and made strenuous, if ultimately unsuccessful, efforts to resolve it. With Hunton, therefore, the argument is far more elaborate and consequently more revealing. Indeed, his *Treatise of Monarchy* and *A Vindication of the Treatise of Monarchy*, which appeared in 1643 and 1644 respectively, contain the most ingenious theory of sovereignty to be published in this period. It is, at the very least, closer than any of the others we have mentioned to an adequate explanation of a mixed constitution.[43]

Although even more extensive, and sometimes more sophisticated, Hunton's view of kingship established by consent is substantially the same as Ferne's. Consent determines the mode and personnel of government, but coercive authority derives from God.[44] Hence the tenure of a limited monarch is granted unconditionally, and cannot be legitimately revoked unless a right of deposition was expressly stipulated.[45] But Ferne, as

send as many as it needs to do the job, and so an army. 'The reason is not the same,' Digges objects, 'because when a few are sent out, the administration doth not endanger the common peace. But because a war doth put the whole kingdom in manifest peril of being ruined when either real delinquents, or pretended to be so, are so many as to make the trial doubtful, the liberty and right of inferior magistrates to fetch them in by force is in this case restrained by express laws which provide very prudently that no war shall be made except authorized by the supreme governor.'

[43] The strength of Hunton as a theorist of public law is now beginning to be recognized. The first modern writer to signalize his merits is C. H. McIlwain, *Constitutionalism and the Changing World* (Cambridge, 1937), pp. 196–231.

[44] Philip Hunton, *A Treatise of Monarchy* (London, 1643), pp. 2–4.

[45] 'If any have been so rash as to hold it [i.e. direct attack on the person or powers of the king] lawful on these grounds, that the whole kingdom is above him because they make him king, and that by miscarriage he may make a forfeiture and so lay himself open to force, I do judge these grounds very insufficient: unless the kingdom reserve a superiority to itself, or there be a fundamental clause of forfeiture on specified causes, and then it is not properly a monarchy' (*ibid.* p. 50).

Hunton rightly notes, becomes inconsistent by refusing to admit resistance. If limitations on the monarch are established by the law and are independent of his will, there must be a sanction to enforce them. For there is no law without a sanction, nor right without a remedy. Nor will it do, as Ferne insists, to say that the limitations are moral rather than juridical, and go to the exercise of power rather than to its root, or fundamental constitution. 'Moral [limitation], since it is no political or authoritative act, makes no real detraction either in the power or the exercise of it and therefore agrees as well to the most absolute government, whereas legal [limitation], being a politic and authoritative act, makes a real diminution, and so is the *ratio formalis*, a distinctive concept, constituting limited government, nor can be found in absolute.'[46]

This principle, moreover, applies to the English kingship also, no matter when the limitations came about. Hunton does not agree that the existing line was originally absolute.[47] But he sees no need to spar with Ferne on that account. Even conceding that the English constitution was the result of 'after-condescent grace,' the royal grant, deliberately and solemnly declared, is like 'a second original constitution,' which has all the force of an original.[48]

But the truly novel step in Hunton, as compared with all the others, is to recognize that the act of resistance, even short of deposition, cannot be an inherent act of public jurisdiction or authority. Were it so, the person or persons vested with that power would be the ultimate locus of sovereign authority, and Hunton's theory of resistance in a limited and in a mixed monarchy is an effort to avoid this outcome.

In this particular context Hunton means by a limited

[46] Philip Hunton, *A Vindication of the Treatise of Monarchy* (London, 1644), p. 27. See also *Treatise*, p. 12.

[47] *Treatise*, pp. 35–7. This is simply the standard argument that William came to England in order to make good a legal claim to the throne. Whether that claim was valid or not, he did not come as a conqueror and did not claim to hold authority as such. Hence the limited monarchy of the Saxon period, which was not overthrown by the Danes, was not destroyed by William either.

[48] *Ibid.* p. 13.

monarchy a system in which power is given to the king alone –
with certain limitations pre-established, but without a representative assembly. This is an odd arrangement, which could
hardly work in practice because it contains no mechanism of
consent to change. But he seems not to be thinking of a work-
ing system. His conception of limited monarchy at this point
seems to be intended mainly as a formal construct designed to
exhibit the nature of resistance in its simplest form.[49]

Hunton begins by positing that 'in a limited legal monarchy
there can be no stated internal judge of the monarch's action,
if there grow a fundamental variance between him and the
community.'[50] But there is a kind of judgment which is not
internal, and which he represents as 'moral' rather than
'authoritative.'

If it [the transgression of law] be mortal and such, as suffered, dissolves
the frame and life of the government and public liberty, then the
illegality and destructive nature is to be set upon and redressment sought
by petition, which, if failing, prevention by resistance ought to be. But
first that it [a transgression tending to destroy the frame of law] is
such as must be made apparent; and if it be apparent and an appeal
made *ad conscientiam generis humani*, especially of those of that community, then the fundamental laws of that monarchy must judge and
pronounce sentence in every man's conscience and every man (as far as
concerns him) must follow the evidence and truth in his own conscience
to oppose or not oppose, [and] according to his conscience acquit or
condemn the act of carriage in the governor.[51]

But Hunton now contends that this procedure is not an act of
authority. It does not import supremacy in the community; or

---

[49] *Vindication*, pp. 22–3. Hunton here asserts that a system can function
without the power to make law so long as its supreme authority may
interpret the established law, and cites the church as an example since its
basic law is established by Scripture. For one fleeting moment he seems to
suggest that, in secular systems, new law may be made if the need is fully
evident. But this does not appear to be his authentic view. In any event
he clearly means that a limited monarchy is 'simple' in the composition of
its sovereign. See *ibid.* p. 21. The same view is advanced with less argument in the *Treatise*.
[50] *Treatise*, p. 17.
[51] *Ibid.* p. 18.

41

any power either to depose the king or to change the form of government:

And this power of judging argues not a superiority in those who judge over him who is judged; for it is not authoritative and civil, but moral, residing in reasonable creatures, and lawful for them to execute because never divested and put off by any act in the constitution of a legal government, but rather the reservation of it intended. For when they define the superior to a law and institute no power to judge of his excesses from that law, it is evident they reserve to themselves not a formal authoritative power, but a moral power, such as they had originally before the constitution of the government, which must needs remain, being not conveyed away in the constitution.[52]

Hunton is correct in holding that this judgment of the community is not internal to the constitution. He is also entitled to call it 'moral' as distinct from 'civil,' since it is not rendered by a specially designated group within the whole acting by pre-established and regular procedures. But it cannot be considered 'moral' as distinguished from 'authoritative' in the sense of 'ultimate' or 'final.' Each person is entitled to pass judgment, not only as to his own right or safety, but as to the right and safety of the entire community of which he is a member. And each person is also entitled to seek execution of his judgment by initiating civil war. The outcome, when all have rendered their decisions and the war is won or lost, is the verdict of the whole community, which must be binding upon all its members. It could not be otherwise, unless we should suppose as an alternative that the community itself had been dissolved and that those composing it had reverted to a state of nature.

On either alternative, allegiance to the king may be withdrawn. But taking the first alternative as being closer to what Hunton had in mind, it is evident, from its right of ultimate and binding judgment, that the community must in some sense be supreme. If it is supreme, then for all the reasons that Hunton has himself provided, it must be entitled to withdraw allegiance and to change the form of government. Yet this conclusion he consistently and strenuously denies, for he agrees

[52] *Ibid.*

42

with Bridge and Burroughs that all interference with the person or office of the king would violate the law of God.[53]

Hunton failed to recognize this difficulty, because he was mainly preparing the ground for his treatment of resistance in a mixed monarchy like the English. In that context the moral judgment of the people, much restricted in its scope, is introduced to qualify and soften, as it were, the civil and authoritative judgment of the Parliament. In this formulation the difficulties of the former notion are less evident and more readily passed over without notice.

By a mixed monarchy Hunton means any constitution in which the king shares powers with a representative body which has an independent right to give or to withhold consent. The term thus applies not only to the English constitution, where the share of Parliament was large, but also to the standard form of European monarchy, in which the power of the king was less than absolute and the consent of the Estates was needed. But even in the English system there is a sense in which the monarch is supreme, despite the element of mixture. The idea of equality among coordinates, which Hunton found in Herle, is explicitly rejected. In any mixture one or another component will predominate, and that component in England is the king. Not only does he have an independent share of the legislative power, but his assent is the final stage in the enactment of a statute; he creates the members of the peerage and determines who among the commons may vote in an election; he is normally empowered to call and to dissolve a Parliament, albeit in accordance with the law; and he alone has executive authority.[54] There is thus a sense in which the legal powers of the English king conform to the standard definition of a

---

[53] '[T]he person of the monarch even in these mixed forms (as I said before in the limited) ought to be above the reach of violence in his utmost exorbitances. For when a people have sworn allegiance and invested a person or line with supremacy, they have made it sacred, and no abuse can divert him of that power irrevocably communicated' (*ibid.* p. 28). Legitimate resistance, then, must be directed against the king's officers. See, for example, *ibid.* p. 52.
[54] *Ibid.* pp. 24–6.

sovereign authority. He gives commands to all – collectively as well as individually – and he takes commands from none.

Hence even in a mixed constitution like the English the king cannot be judged by a regularly constituted power, for he does not acknowledge an equal, let alone a superior authority.[55] Hence Hunton's first formulation of the procedure for resistance in a kingship mixed sounds much the same as a kingship limited:

One inconvenience must necessarily be in all mixed governments, which I showed to be in limited governments. There can be no constituted legal authoritative judge of the fundamental controversies arising betwixt the three estates. If such do arise, it is the fatal disease of these governments for which no salve can be prescribed. For the established being of such authority would *ipso facto* overthrow the frame and turn it into absoluteness; so that if one of these, or two, say their power is invaded and the government assaulted in the other, the accused denying it, it doth become a controversy. Of this question, there is no legal judge. It is a case beyond the possible provision of such a government. The accusing side must make it evident to every man's conscience. In this case, which is beyond the government, the appeal must be made to the community as if there were no government, and as by evidence men's consciences are convinced, they are bound to give their utmost assistance. For the intention of the frame in such a state justifies the exercise of any power conducing to the safety of the universality and the government established.[56]

But by a subtle change in phrasing, the power of the people has now been radically diminished. The people no longer has the power to initiate. It is merely called upon to arbitrate a conflict that has been initiated by the king or Parliament – to decide which side is right and to give assistance accordingly. In reply to Ferne's complaint that appeal to the community 'as if there were no government' opens up a path to anarchy, Hunton makes this point explicit. 'I say not simply that the people are

[55] But Hunton's argument is generalized for any mixture, even one in which the components are completely equal. This is clearly indicated in his critique of Herle (*ibid.* pp. 71–2). He denies the right of substitution by the two houses on the grounds that it destroys the mixture of the constitution, even conceding Herle's representation of it.
[56] *Ibid.* p. 29.

at liberty as if there were no government, but only in this particular question, bound still, as before, in all besides.'[57]

By this restriction the implication of constituent authority seems to be removed. Yet Hunton's solution serves only to complicate the issue. If on the one hand, the people is free to choose at all, it must be entitled to initiate resistance of its own in order to secure its safety, and, in pursuit of that objective, to depose the king and even to change the form of government. But if, on the other hand, the people is bound 'absolutely' to government by king and Parliament, as Hunton frequently insists,[58] it has reserved no capacity to act, and could not even make choice of whom it would support.

The same difficulty reappears, inevitably, in Hunton's inability to account for the legal force of measures taken by the Parliament. An act like the Militia Ordinance – or any act requiring the subject to give help – is an invocation of authority. If the subject is obligated to obey by law, then Parliament is supreme within the constitution. If the subject is free in law (if not necessarily in conscience) to choose the other side, he has no legal obligation and the initiative of Parliament is not an authoritative legal act at all. What Hunton seeks is to combine an authoritative act by Parliament, in order to keep ultimate power from the people, with free decision by the people, in order to keep ultimate power from the Parliament. But the notion of a non-binding authoritative act is contradictory. Either the people or the Parliament must be supreme.

It is this second difficulty which finally brings Hunton back to Bridge and Burroughs. If the measures of resistance enacted by the Parliament were officially binding in any sense at all, as Hunton genuinely thinks,[59] then there is a right of final judgment in the Parliament that falls within the constitution and

---

[57] *Vindication*, p. 49.
[58] This follows in all of the many statements that, absent a specific clause of forfeiture, power once given is irrevocable. See, for example, *Treatise*, p. 16. Furthermore, in discussing the question of resistance in respect to the English constitution, Hunton goes out of his way to say that 'all three [estates of Parliament] together are absolute and equivalent to the power of the most absolute monarch' (*ibid.* p. 61).   [59] But see below p. 48, n. 68.

contradicts the principle of monarchy. Desperately attempting to avoid this outcome, Hunton sometimes speaks of self-defense.[60] Since the right of Parliament is independent of the king's authority, it must be inherently entitled to defend that right from usurpation. This approach could have been suggested by remarks in Grotius, whose work was widely admired by educated Englishmen. But in Grotius the right of self-defense by one of two partners in a mixed constitution is a right of war. It thus entails, as Grotius indicates, a right in the winner, if his cause is just, to expropriate the power of the other as a punishment, in accordance with the laws of war.[61] Hunton, seeking to stop short of this, would have the right of self-defense in Parliament to be a limited power within the constitution. He is thus at last obliged to go down the very path that had been officially taken by the Parliament itself. The Militia Ordinance, he says, is not law 'formally,' yet it is law 'eminently' – which is a distinction without a difference since, however extraordinary the occasion for its exercise, it is described by Hunton as a power within the constitution. The two houses, he says, 'may by extraordinary and temporary ordinance assume the arms wherewith the king is trusted and perform the king's trust.' The Militia Ordinance, indeed, is not even a temporary violation of the king's authority since it is in accord with his 'deliberate' as distinguished from his 'sudden' will.[62]

In the *Vindication*, however, Hunton makes one further effort to explain the authority of Parliament without appealing to the right of substitution. Pursuing a thought which is hinted at briefly in the *Treatise* and which we have already seen in Bridge,[63] he now compares the Militia Ordinance to the raising of a *posse comitatus*. Just as a sheriff in the county could raise its power against those who defied its jurisdiction, so Parlia-

---

[60] *Ibid.* pp. 28, 76. The right of self-defense is not supported by any particular principle of law. It is said to follow from the very end of a mixed constitution, which is to check usurpation by the king.
[61] For the remarks of Grotius on this point and also of Christopher Besold (by whom Hunton was probably also influenced), see below p. 68.
[62] *Treatise*, pp. 62–3.
[63] *Ibid.* p. 56.

ment could raise the *posse regni,* or power of the kingdom.[64]
In English law, moreover, the power of the sheriff and the
county court extended not only to ordinary subjects but to royal
officers claiming to act upon the king's command. Parliament,
accordingly, could use all the force it needed against all those
officers and soldiers, assembled at the king's command, who,
wittingly or not, were the instruments of his illegal design to
introduce an arbitrary government. The power of resistance,
says Hunton, is in 'the courts of justice, and especially the
supreme court to whom the conservation of government and
law is committed, and a power not only to resist, but also
censure and punish its violators, much more its subverters
without regard to number or warrant.'[65]

One difficulty here is that the county sheriff is empowered
to pursue delinquents by the king's commission, which Parliament did not possess. But even so the analogy is overdrawn.
The *posse comitatus* is directed against particular delinquents
charged with particular acts of defiance, and also against those
persons who deliberately aid them in defiance. But the power
raised by Parliament was generally directed at any and all
persons who served the king in any way and thereby contributed
support to his authority. This, Ferne had said, is assumption of
'the power';[66] and Hunton, fully grasping the force of this
objection, is ultimately driven to invoke the right of substitution. 'The forces of the sovereign in truth are the forces raised
to defend his government, not those which are raised to subvert
it. They are his, which have his authoritative will, not those
which have only his arbitrary.'[67]

Hunton, then, came close to a solution that he never fully

[64] This legal analogy was often used at the time. Apart from Bridge, it also
appears in Henry Parker, *A Political Catechism* (London, 1643), p. 10 and
in Herle, *Fuller Answer,* p. 10. The term *posse regni* (which Hunton does
not use expressly) appears in both of the latter two.
[65] *Vindication,* p. 68.
[66] 'The argument from the process of inferior courts or from the Parliament's
power to resist and commit such private men assaulting them, is altogether
inconsequent to prove their power to raise armies and by them to oppose
the forces of their sovereign...' (*Reply to Several Treatises,* p. 96).
[67] *Ibid.* p. 69.

reached. He clearly saw that in a mixed constitution none of the partners in sovereign authority can claim an inherent right of final judgment. He also saw that judgment by the general community is not an act of civil jurisdiction that falls within the constitution. But the essential step that Hunton fails to take is to make the judgment of the people final and authoritative. He simply cannot see that constituent power in the people, as distinguished from the Parliament, is not incompatible with monarchy. In his view the possessor of that power, no matter who it is, must be 'above' the king in every sense. This error, confirmed by his fear of revolution, leads him to complete elimination of constituent authority. But it cannot be eliminated; in consequence Hunton is finally driven to abandon all that is valuable in his conception of a mixed constitution. With much reluctance, and yet with no alternative, he assigns that power confusedly to Parliament.[68]

[68] It was not so much than Hunton, a legal thinker of extraordinary subtlety, failed to see the difficulty. It was rather that he simply could not see a way of solving it. The following passage nicely indicates the depth of the problem for writers of the seventeenth century:

> If any wonder I should justify a power in the two houses to resist, and command aids against any agents of destructive commands of the king, and yet not allow them power of judging when these agents or commands are destructive, I answer: I do not simply deny them power of judging and declaring this; but I deny them to be a legal court ordained to judge of this case authoritatively, so as to bind all people to receive and rest in their judgment for conscience of its authority and because they [the two houses] have voted it. 'Tis the evidence, not the power of their votes [that] must bind our reason and practice in this case. We ought to conceive their votes and discoveries [to be] made by the best eyes of the kingdom, and which in likelihood should see most. But when they vote a thing against the proceedings of a third and [at least equally] supreme estate, our consciences must have evidence of truth to guide them, and not the sole authority of votes...' (*Treatise*, p. 73).

Hunton thus recognizes that the measures taken by Parliament, as he understands them, are, at once, acts of jurisdiction yet also less than binding. The inconsistency, presumably, seemed so ultimate to him that he felt entitled to state it as a kind of paradoxical truth about resistance in a mixed constitution.

I feel justified, however, in having said that Hunton tended to resolve this paradox in favor of Parliament's authority. This is already suggested

The Parliamentary publicists of the early 1640s were thus unable to arrive at a theory of resistance consistent with a mixed constitution. One group was able to legitimate resistance by premising constituent authority in Parliament, but it could not account for the independence of the king, which it somehow wished to maintain. The other group could account for royal independence by denying constituent authority, but it could not, consistent with this premise, explain how resistance could ever be legitimate.

We should also observe, albeit briefly, that these difficulties, already noted by the royalists, would be even more glaringly exposed in some of the debates that followed upon the introduction of the Commonwealth. In the early 1640s, the two versions of Parliamentary theory just examined had been compatible politically. The proponents of constituent authority did not anticipate removal of the king and perhaps thought they had excluded it in principle. Those who proceeded from royal sacrosanctity, on the other hand, managed to endorse all the measures taken by the Parliament. At the beginning, therefore, the competing interpretations were but two different ways of arriving at the same result. But by the end of the decade they would be ranged against each other.

The revolution of 1649 was enacted by the more militant minority of the House of Commons, generally known as Independents, who were given power, and sustained in power, by the army. In December 1648 the moderate majority,

by the constant emphasis of the *Treatise* on the jurisdiction of the Parliament as distinct from the initiative of private individuals. But it is clearly indicated by the tone of the *Vindication*, which is represented by some of the passages quoted in the text. See above pp. 46–7. Hunton had been bitterly attacked by Ferne for having seemed to admit the initiation of resistance by private individuals. And Hunton responds in the *Vindication* by eliminating that principle almost completely. The basis of resistance is now the right of the two houses considered as the highest court to raise the *posse regni*. The individual is presumably bound to go along, although Hunton does not say so in so many words. The outcome, therefore, is the assertion of Parliamentary supremacy with respect to all measures short of deposition. But that reservation has no more foundation now in Hunton, than it has in Bridge or Burroughs.

generally known as Presbyterians, was forcibly secluded from the house by the regiments of Colonel Pride, and the members still remaining now deliberately proceeded to enact a revolution. In January 1649, the Rump of the House of Commons erected an extraordinary tribunal, without the Lords' consent, which tried and executed Charles I for treason. In March the monarchy was formally abolished together with the House of Lords. And on May 19, 1649, England was declared a Commonwealth – without a king or House of Lords. The House of Commons was thus left in sole possession of ultimate juridical authority.

The official legal doctrine of the Commonwealth was a radicalized version of the thesis of constituent power as we have encountered it in Parker, Herle, and Prynne. Since the House of Commons was alone the people's representative, it had all the powers of an English Parliament, and was thus entitled to depose the king and to change the constitution on its unilateral finding of an urgent public need. And since this finding was an act of jurisdiction, it was fully binding on the individual and could not be questioned in any other court.

Even conceding the premise of this argument, the conclusion clearly did not follow. The body in whose name the revolution was enacted was not an authentic House of Commons, but an illegally constituted Rump. A few adherents of the Commonwealth tried to brazen out this difficulty on the grounds that the members purged in December 1648 had been subsequently invited to return.[69] But the condition of return, as the Presbyterians properly objected, was subscription to a number of revolutionary decisions, none of which had been adopted by a legal house.[70]

We may also note that this initial defect of consent was never to be subsequently repaired. The English political nation might have been willing to accept a monarchy without the

[69] See, for example, Samuel Eaton, *The Oath of Allegiance and the National Covenant Proved to be Non-obliging*...(London, 1650), p. 4, and also *Memorandums of the Conferences Held Between Brethren*, London, 1650, pp. 32–5.
[70] Edward Gee, *A Vindication of the Oath of Allegiance*...(n.p. 1650), p. 41, and among many others, Prynne, *Summary Reasons*, p. 12.

Stuart dynasty.[71] But it was adamantly opposed to a republic.
The Rump did not dissolve and call a new election. After it was
dismissed in 1653, none of the Parliaments subsequently called
by Cromwell could be permitted to meet without controls.
Either the members were not elected freely, or else the persons
returned by the constituencies were not allowed to take their
seats unless they passed a test of loyalty imposed on the house
by the executive.

Hence on any doctrine of consent whatever, the new regime
was illegitimate, and this was the most common and most
persuasive objection raised by its Presbyterian opponents. But
for many, this was not enough. To admit that revolution could
have been legitimate, if only it were rightly done, seemed to be
a dangerous concession; for the Independents accused their
former allies of having betrayed the common cause by refusing
to endorse the final step. The need for such a final step could
be denied, of course, on the grounds of prudence, respect for
law and former promises, and the advantage of kingship to the
English public. But the most iron-clad defense of all, if only its
premises were granted, was to hold that revolution was illegitimate as such. And many Presbyterian opponents of the new
regime thus invoked the principle of royal sacrosanctity, more
or less as we have seen it in Burroughs, Bridge, and Hunton, in
order to show that legitimate resistance must stop short of
deposition.

One strand, then, in the controversies that followed on the
revolution was a confrontation between the thesis of limited
resistance and that of the constituent power of the people's
representative. The exchange between the Presbyterian, Edward
Gee, and the Independent, Samuel Eaton – both of them formidable controversialists – was one of the most brilliant of this
period.

There is no reason to review the details of this exchange,[72]

[71] Edward Hyde, Earl of Clarendon, *The History of the Rebellion and Civil
Wars in England*, 6 vols. (Oxford, 1888), VI, 21–2.
[72] Gee's *Vindication* started the exchange by criticizing a brief letter by Eaton
published without his consent (*Oath of Allegiance*), and Eaton then replied

since the arguments significant for present purposes have already been presented. But we may observe that the net result was utter impasse. Gee could show, with devastating force, that the thesis of the supremacy of Parliament in general and of the House of Commons in particular – no matter what else its difficulties as applied to the events of 1649 – was hopelessly at odds with any sensible interpretation of the historic English constitution. On the other hand, Eaton could show, with equally devastating force, that the thesis of royal sacrosanctity had been consistently contradicted by the measures of resistance that the Presbyterians had themselves endorsed in 1642.

to this criticism in his *Reply to an Answer Pretending to Refute Some Positions which Tended to Make the Oath of Allegiance Void and Non-obliging.*

3

George Lawson

AN ADEQUATE SOLUTION to the problem of resistance in a mixed
monarchy was finally to appear in George Lawson's *Politica
sacra et civilis*, which was completed by 1657, although its
publication was accidentally delayed until 1660. As the title
indicates, the work is a comprehensive treatise on the basic
principles of ecclesiastical and civil government. In the chapters
on the state, which take up roughly half the book, Lawson at
last concludes that the government of England had been dissolved in 1642 and that all of its powers had legally reverted to
the general community.[1]

[1] Lawson's published works, in the order of their appearance, are: *An
Examination of the Political Part of Mr. Hobbes his Leviathan* (London,
1657); *Theo-Politica: or a Body of Divinity*...(London, 1659); *Politica
sacra et civilis*...(London, 1660); *An Exposition of the Epistle to the
Hebrews* (London, 1662); *Magna Charta ecclesiae universalis*...(2nd ed.
London, 1686). No first edition of this work is listed either in the Wing
Catalogue or in the British Museum Printed Catalogue. The National Union
Catalog of pre-1956 imprints lists what is probably a first edition (London,
1665) at the William Andrews Clark Memorial Library, University of
California at Los Angeles. A *Catalogus librorum* is listed under Lawson's
name in Wing (no. 705) but it is actually a catalog of books offered for
auction by Edward Millington, in which books from the libraries of Lawson
and of three other persons are collected. Mr. Philip Spurling of the Grolier
Club library was kind enough to locate a copy of that *Catalogus* in the
Grolier collection, and it turns out to be of no value in determining what
Lawson may have owned.
    The first modern scholar to call attention to Lawson's political thought
and to show its similarities to Locke's is A. H. Maclean, 'George Lawson
and John Locke,' *Cambridge Historical Journal*, IX, no. 1 (1947), 68–77, in
which he also assays what details exist on Lawson's biography. See also
'The Origins of the Political Opinions of John Locke' (unpublished doctoral
dissertation, Cambridge University, 1947), ch. IV and especially appendix II.

Lawson was a conforming cleric who had supported Parliament in 1642. Most Episcopalian clergymen, faced with a House of Commons in which Presbyterian influence was strong, had clung to the cause of Charles I, whose policy, at least as it was publicly professed, promised defense of the Established Church. Lawson, however, was an unusual but by no means isolated exception. Liberal in his theology and genuinely irenic in his disposition, he sincerely believed that with enough good will all the more respectable tendencies in English Protestantism could be comprehended in a single establishment. Governance by bishops could be associated with forms of election and a council of elders to accommodate the Presbyterians, and substantial autonomy accorded to local congregations might even accommodate the Independents. A major theme of the *Politica sacra et civilis* is a principled defense of this solution.[2] It was presumably in this spirit that Lawson took the Solemn League and Covenant of 1643, which envisaged church reform. He later complained that the measures that followed were too radical. But this he blamed on pressure from the Scots.[3] As late as 1660 he continued to believe that comprehension would succeed once the English people became free to act upon their wishes.

Lawson, then, took no ecclesiastical position that prevented his support of Parliament. We may assume that he embraced its cause on much the same judgment of events that he was to advance in 1657. The civil war was a defense of the English constitution against the design of Charles to introduce an arbitrary government; it was also a defense of the Protestant religion against a design to reimpose Catholicism.[4]

An account of Lawson as a critic of Hobbes is John Bowles, *Hobbes and His Critics* (London, 1951), pp. 86–100. Neither account deals with the relationship of Lawson's doctrine to the problem of resistance in a mixed constitution.

[2] George Lawson, *Politica sacra et civilis* (2nd ed. London, 1689), pp. 349–51. I have used the second edition because it is more readily available. I have checked that edition against the first of 1660 and find that it differs only in pagination.

[3] *Ibid.* pp. 177–8.

[4] *Ibid.* pp. 171–6.

Although all of this is fairly clear, we are completely un-informed as to what Lawson considered, in 1642, to be the legal justification of resistance. I shall suppose, however – since there is no reason to think otherwise – that he simply accepted the official claims of Parliament. The civil war was thus con-ducted by the constitutional authority of Parliament to protect the public safety.[5] But it would not extend to alteration of the kingship or removal of the king either because Parliament lacked that power under English law or because it had solemnly promised not to use it. I shall also suppose, finally, that in the later 1640s Lawson was sympathetic to the moderate party in the House of Commons, which is generally known as 'Presbyterian.' He would thus have held that the English constitution must be settled with the king's consent, which would ultimately be given if Parliament were patient and persistent.

Throughout the 1640s, therefore, Lawson's views were prob-ably standard. But the events of 1649 were now to lead him down a solitary path. Up to a certain point his reaction to the revolution of that year was characteristic of moderate opinion. For him, as for most others who had supported Parliament in 1642, the new regime was a mere usurpation of authority. It had originated in the purge of the House of Commons in December 1648, which was an illegal act of force. And neither the Commonwealth nor the Protectorate was to be ratified by a free expression of consent. The moderates, moreover, would not admit that the revolution and its outcome were dictated by political necessity or the positive decree of providence.[6] They continued to believe that a peaceful settlement had been possible

[5] I am assuming, therefore, that Lawson was closer to the thesis of con-stituent authority rather than to Hunton's thesis. I find no hint that he ever held the latter view or that he even took it seriously. For reasons that will be more evident later, I suspect that he would have been closest to Prynne's version of the constituent thesis. But he need not have had a fully reasoned theory at that time. His leanings toward constituent authority would most likely have been mere acquiescence in the official position of the Parliament in which that theme is strong.

[6] Lawson, in 1657, reflects that the fate of Charles I was in accord with the providence of God (*ibid.* p. 96). But he does not hold, as many Indepen-

in 1648. In any event the protection of the English people and the Protestant religion did not require a republic.

Beyond this point, Lawson's opinion was divergent. Most moderates now went into opposition and supported the claims of Charles II. They argued that, since Charles I had not been lawfully removed, nor the office of the kingship lawfully abolished, Charles II had automatically succeeded on his father's death. Furthermore, since the lawful Parliament had been suppressed and its membership dispersed, the cause of lawful government was now visibly upheld by Charles alone. A subject loyal to the constitution thus seemed bound in conscience to uphold the cause of Charles II. For some Presbyterians, like Christopher Love, this meant active participation in royalist conspiracies. But for most, like Richard Baxter, it meant little more than calm and unprovocative insistence on the legitimacy of Charles' title.[7]

Lawson, however, was among that smaller but still numerous group of moderates who collaborated with the new regime and repudiated Charles II. For many of these, no doubt, the real motive was timidity or opportunism.[8] But some at least, including Lawson, were deeply persuaded that cooperation with the new regime, even though its power was usurped, was by far the lesser of two evils.

To support the cause of Charles against the Commonwealth was to encourage yet another civil war, and, even worse, to invite an invasion by the Scots. From 1650 until his defeat in 1651, Charles' strategy hinged upon the Scots. At the time of

dents, that the revolution had been authorized by a positive mandate of providence.

    This more radical position does not concern us here. Lawson belongs to those whom J. G. A. Pocock would call, in contrast, casuists. For that distinction, as applied to the revolutionary period as a whole, see J. G. A. Pocock, 'The Political Thought of the Cromwellian Interregnum,' in G. A. Wood and P. S. O'Connor (eds.), *W. P. Morrell: A Tribute* (Dunedin, (1973); and also his introduction to his *Political Works of James Harrington* (Cambridge, 1977).

[7] Richard Baxter, *Reliquiae Baxterianae*, ed. Matthew Sylvester (London, 1696), Part I, pp. 71–2.

[8] For the standard position of these 'Presbyterian engagers' see below p. 62.

the second civil war in 1648 it had also been the strategy of certain Presbyterian members of Parliament, and Lawson, looking back, later described it as an act of treason.[9] For if the Scots had prevailed against the English army, which was then the army of the Independents and, later, of the Commonwealth, the people of England would have had to suffer many of the afflictions of a conquered nation.[10] But even greater horrors would impend if Charles should conquer with the Scots and then attempt to free himself of their influence. Presbyterians had once believed that Charles I had planned to subdue England with the Irish and perhaps the French. That, indeed, was the very menace that had decided them for civil war. Yet Charles II, whose Catholic sympathies were more overt, was even more likely than his father to fall back upon that course. The danger, at worst, was not only foreign conquest and arbitrary government, but extirpation of the Protestant religion. The danger, at its least, was that a prostrate England would become a battlefield for foreign armies – with the Protestant Scots on the one side, and the Cavalier and foreign Catholic forces on the other. The English would then be exposed to all the horrors suffered by the Germans in the course of the Thirty Years' War.[11]

After the conquest of Scotland in 1651, such menaces became less imminent, which perhaps explains why Lawson, in

[9] *Politics*, pp. 180–1.

[10] Thus in the *Memorandums of the Conferences*, p. 35, those ministers, who wanted to withhold allegiance to the Commonwealth until a proper House of Commons could pass judgment, are warned that while 'they too much hold forth such a principle to bring in another government, they do unadvisedly and against their own good meaning strengthen the hands of some others who seek to undermine and overthrow both this and that form of government, and in stead thereof either drop the nation into a most certain and perfect state of slavery upon the account of conquest, or drown the nation in anarchy and confusion.'

[11] The anonymous author of *England's Apology for its Late Change* (London, 1651), p. 32, believes that England would have become another Germany were it not for the intervention of the army in 1648: '[L]et Germany's example be an occasion to think on the king and the Scots, while we slight the mention of the Commonwealth which God hath given us all advantages to make, not only sure, but the first and choicest in Europe.'

1657, does not spell them out. Yet almost to the very end of the Interregnum, it seemed obvious to all that Charles II could not come back to England without another civil war and the introduction of a foreign army. And Lawson warns that the national interest of England and the cause of Protestantism – not only at home but possibly in all of Europe – might suffer fatal injury unless well-affected Protestants cooperated with the present government.[12]

The new regime, moveover, was soon revealed to be far less radical than the moderates at first had feared. In 1649 Cromwell and the Independent officers around him broke with the Levellers and suppressed the army radicals, in clear rejection of a democratic revolution. Numerous moderates had been exempted from the purge of 1648, and as secluded members gradually returned – after making the required declarations – the power of the moderates increased. So slow was the movement of the Rump in reforming legal institutions and revising the election law that the army Independents were themselves offended.[13] But most welcome of all, from the standpoint of the moderate clergy, was the Rump's restraint in its religious policy. While it hesitantly granted religious toleration, and did not suppress the sectarians completely – policies of which Lawson disapproved[14] – it did not insist on the full program of the Independents, which was complete separation of the church and state. Livings held in the establishment, now mostly in the hands of Presbyterians, were generally left intact.[15] And legislation which required attendance at church in some form or other and which regulated public morals, was prosecuted with unprecedented vigor. For a Presbyterian Puritan like Richard Baxter this stance was so refreshing that he was even tempted to relax his opposition.[16]

But the most welcome trend of policy for Lawson was the

---

[12] *Politica*, Epistle to the Reader.
[13] See Blair Worden, *The Rump Parliament* (Cambridge, 1974), ii, 8.
[14] *Politica*, p. 181.
[15] Worden, *Rump Parliament*, ii, 7.
[16] *Reliquiae*, Part i, pp. 87, 100.

George Lawson

subsequent movement of the new regime toward piecemeal restoration of many features of the former constitution. Mixed monarchy, highly diluted, was the form of government that Lawson personally preferred. But quite apart from preference, and more important in his calculations, was his judgment, which turned out to be correct, that this was the only form of government on which the English people could be freely settled.[17] He did not believe – here too, perhaps, correctly – that the Stuarts had to be restored, and he clearly looked to their exclusion.[18] He also thought that the kingship should be made elective, to preclude the succession of a Catholic to the throne;[19] and he may have wanted some modification in the powers and composition of the House of Lords.[20] But these were merely tentative suggestions made in passing. Lawson's

[17] *Politica*, p. 190. 'The foundation to be laid out is, first to find out the ancient constitution before it was corrupted too much, and understand the great wisdom of our ancestors, gained by long experience in the constitution of this state...It's a vain and presumptuous imagination to think we have attained to a greater measure of wisdom than our ancestors attained unto. And let us not undo what is already done, if it be consistent with the best model.'

And so also in the reply to Hobbes (*An Examination*, p. 44): 'To endeavor a change in a quiet state, and that out of ambition, or a high conceit of their own state-learning, will much offend God and bring great misery on man. Alterations in government, which though they be for the better, if sudden, are dangerous, and should be made insensibly and by little and little – yet so, that if there be anything in the former old constitution, which is good, it should be retained...' This passage goes on, as if to illustrate the point, by suggesting that the 'common law' be 'introduced' to provide a 'wonderful compendium' in the sense of a more coherent code. It is not clear here whether Lawson is thinking of suggestions, put forward in the Interregnum, for codification of the English common law, or of the Roman civil law in the sense of the *jus commune* of Europe. Since this passage is isolated, I see no way to decide. The confusion of the passage may also result from an error in the text or in the printing, of which there are many in the *Politica*, although relatively few in *An Examination*.

[18] *Politica*, pp. 93–4.

[19] *Ibid*. pp. 190–1.

[20] There is a suggestion that membership in the House of Lords might be made to go by merit rather than descent (*Politica*, p. 398). On possible reduction of its legislative powers by including the peers together with the commons in a single chamber, see below p. 75.

59

central thought was that some version of the ancient constitution was the only form of settlement that the English people would willingly accept.

This possibility seemed not to be precluded by cooperation with the new regime. The revolution of 1649 had preserved at least the format of a House of Commons. By the end of 1653, Cromwell, who had always been partial to a strong executive, was made Protector and there was much talk of a mixed and balanced constitution.[21] But by 1657 the signs of vitality in the older institutions must have seemed particularly strong. At the time of the Humble Petition and Advice, which Lawson mentions with approval,[22] Cromwell's House of Commons petitioned him to take the kingship. His reluctant refusal could be readily interpreted as temporary; and even so, the constitution of the Protectorate was revised to include an upper, or 'other' house.[23] It must have seemed to Lawson, then, that the drift toward a reformed version of the ancient constitution was inexorable – if only existing tendencies were left to take their course. He could have come to this opinion by the mid-1650s, and even earlier perhaps, since the idea of the Protectorate as an initial step toward monarchy was probably widespread in Lawson's circle of acquaintances.

Lawson thus concluded at some point that collaboration with the new regime was the surest method, consistent with the public safety, of returning to a settled government. Quite apart from the other dangers we have mentioned, there were additional reasons why the pace of change should not be rushed. The English public was still fragmented by the party struggles of the civil wars and Interregnum. It was confused and uncertain as to the meaning of its former constitution, the very shape of which had been obscured, and almost lost, by the many distortions introduced since 1642.[24] Above all, the English nation was not yet cured of its self-destructive attach-

[21] Ivan Roots, *Commonwealth and Protectorate* (New York, 1966), p. 171.
[22] *Ibid.* p. 186. The offer of the royal title in the first version of the Petition was, of course, modified at Cromwell's request.
[23] *Ibid.* p. 222.
[24] *Politica*, p. 190.

ment to the Stuart dynasty.[25] In Lawson's judgment, agreement on the constitution, and on an alternative to Charles II in the kingship, would have to be accomplished step by step as the existing government evolved. It would thus be essential to support the present power and to work for transformation from within.

But the moral problem for Lawson, as for other moderates willing to cooperate, was how to justify support of a usurper. His initial response to this question was formed, sometime around 1650, during the controversy over taking the Engagement, or pledge of allegiance, to the Commonwealth.[26] Lawson recommended taking it. In some papers that he showed to Richard Baxter and perhaps to other clergymen as well, he probably rested almost his entire case upon the 'fact' of conquest. The English people, subdued by overwhelming force, was entitled to surrender on whatever terms it could obtain, and to submit to all commands not inconsistent with the law of God.[27] To persist in opposition would only worsen its con-

[25] *Ibid.* p. 383.

[26] The Engagement, first enacted in October 1649, went through several revisions as to language and the persons required to take it. In its final form of January 1650, all adult males were required, under severe penalties, to take the following pledge: 'I do declare and promise that I shall be true and faithful to the Commonwealth of England as the same is now established without a king and House of Lords.' The propriety of taking this pledge was the formal issue in the debate between the Presbyterians and Independents.

[27] 'Also I have seen,' says Baxter, 'some ingenious manuscripts of his for the taking of the Engagement (to be true to the Commonwealth as established without a king and House of Lords), his opinion being much for submission to the present possessor though a usurper. But I thought these papers easily answerable.' These papers are clearly distinct from the *Politica* since that work is mentioned by Baxter in the preceding sentence (*Reliquiae*, Part I, p. 108).

The right of a people to surrender to a conqueror is defended in *Politica*, p. 93. Although not very common among the 'Presbyterian Engagers,' the idea of surrender in the public interest is sometimes found among them, as for example in S.W., *The Constant Man's Character* (London, 1650), and also in the anonymous, *Conscience Puzzled* (n.p. 1650). For reasons to be given later (see below p. 129), I am inclined to think that Lawson would have published the papers that he showed to Baxter and that his position was much the same as in *Conscience Puzzled*. Indeed, given certain

dition. Thus no individual was entitled to uphold the cause of Charles II even if he wished to do so. His duty to the English people overrode all obligation to his former governors.[28]

As compared with the other formulae devised by the moderate engagers, Lawson's solution preserved the rights of the community except in the most extraordinary circumstances. The most common way of justifying the Engagement among moderates was to find a duty to usurpers in the obligation of a Christian to be subject to the higher powers. Another, which started from individual self-preservation as the highest moral principle, inferred a right and duty to accept an offer of protection from any possessor of effective power.[29] But at least

> similarities of style and some anticipation of other points in the *Politica*, it is even possible that *Conscience Puzzled* was the published version of the papers shown to Baxter. In any event, in that pamphlet the case for surrender is as follows (p. 8):
>
>> In case of conquest when an overruling power (by force of arms or otherwise) shall conquer a nation and render, as well the people unable to maintain their former government and governors, as the governors to defend and protect their people in pursuit of their oaths, covenants, and obligations to them; then we count it lawful for a people to make the best conditions they can with the conquerors, to desire protection from them, and promise subjection to them. And the reason is, because all former obligation either of the governors to the governed or the governed to the governors, did extend no farther than the power of the obliged on both parts. Which power in both parties being, by a total conquest, overcome by a third party; the obligation to the mutual exercise of that power must cease, because the power itself is ceased. . .
>>
>> This case, if it be ours – and it is declared, avowed, and owned that we are a conquered nation – we are ready to make the best conditions we can for ourselves. And the former power (under the shadow whereof we breathed) being vanished whilst we cry quarter and look for protection from the succeeding power, we declare that we will be true and faithful in all things whereby we may not draw upon ourselves the guilt of disobedience to God.

[28] *Politica*, pp. 89–90.
[29] The earliest and most influential presentation of the first approach is Francis Rous, *The Lawfulness of Obeying the Present Government* (London, 1649). The most impressive statement of the second is by Anthony Ascham, especially in *The Bounds and Bonds of our Public Obedience* (London, 1649).

Both views of course are often intertwined in any given writer. For a

George Lawson

from a constitutionalist standpoint the consequences were grotesque. On either view forcible resistance to a tyrant was excluded altogether, at least when it was undertaken on behalf of the community. The individual, furthermore, was not obliged to take risks for the sake of the community. In any conflict he was free to transfer his allegiance to that party which seemed stronger at the time. With Lawson, on the other hand, the community would continue in its rights, and individuals would be required to uphold them, until the nation as a whole became subject to force that was clearly overwhelming.

But precisely for this reason, Lawson's argument could not achieve his goal, which was to persuade his fellow moderates to desist from their support of Charles. The cause of restoration, the Presbyterians objected, was far from being hopeless,[30] and this was a plausible contention. Throughout the Interregnum Charles II actively contested the power of the new regime. In 1651 he had suffered a serious setback as a result of his defeat in Scotland. As the new government became more stable he found it increasingly difficult to obtain aid from other foreign sources. Yet even so his cause was not quixotic. A numerous party supported him in England. Foreign aid, although uncertain, was always a distinct possibility, and would even be likely in the event of a serious domestic rising. The intransigents could thus contend that the English were still obliged to Charles II. The individual was bound, moreover, to uphold his cause not only because of what he owed to Charles, but in order to defend the right of his community to have a government to which it had consented.

succinct and lucid account of the main theoretical issues see Quentin Skinner, 'Conquest and Consent,' in G. E. Aylmer (ed.), *The Interregnum* (Hamden, Conn., 1972), pp. 79–98. John M. Wallace, 'The Engagement Controversy, 1649–52,' *Bulletin of the New York Public Library*, LXVIII (1964), pp. 384–405, provides a list of pamphlets, each judiciously summarized, along with an introductory essay on the literature and the problem. An extended history of the Engagement controversy forms the largest part of Linda Marasco, *'De Facto* Obligation: Historical and Theoretical Perspectives' (unpublished doctoral dissertation, Columbia University, 1977).

[30] The claim is standard, but see, for instance, Edward Gee, *An Exercitation*

63

Lawson, sensitive to such objections, must soon have recognized that more argument was needed. Sometime in the early 1650s he came to see that he had to show the opposition moderates that legal obligation to their former governors had been terminated independently and antecedently – without regard to the coup of 1648. He came to this conclusion in the only way he could, considering the facts. He now contended that in strictest law the government of England had been dissolved in 1642 by the conflict between king and Parliament. At that point all political authority had technically reverted to the people. The individual Englishman might thus be free to collaborate with the present power, notwithstanding its dependence on force, and might even be obliged to do so in consideration of the public interest.

In order to arrive at this conclusion Lawson now distinguished the constituent power, or 'real majesty,' of the general community from the 'personal,' or ordinary, power of the two houses of Parliament which it had exercised conjointly with the king. Although Lawson's terminology was old, this application of it was completely new.

The terms real and personal majesty pertained to the ownership and use of sovereignty, and that distinction – although not the terminology – had already been used by monarchomach writers of the early seventeenth century.[31] The powers given to the prince were deemed to be a usufruct or use, since possession of them was subject to prescribed conditions. The sovereignty of the people, on the other hand, being ultimate, inherent, and inalienable, was represented as a right of ownership.[32] But in

---

Concerning Usurped Powers (n.p. 1650), pp. 75–6, and also his *Plea for Non-Subscribers*...(n.p. 1650), p. 41 and Appendix, p. 31.

[31] In the sixteenth century the idea is less distinct. But Theodore Beza, in his *Right of Magistrates*, describes the king as holding of the kingdom and standing in relation to it as a feudal vassal to his lord (Julian H. Franklin, *Constitutionalism and Resistance in the Sixteenth Century* (New York, 1969), p. 128), and the distinction between use and ownership of power by the king is also developed in the *Vindiciae contra tyrannos* (*ibid.* pp. 173–4).

[32] Thus Johannes Althusius: '[The] supreme magistrate is he who has been

monarchomach usage, the rights of ownership were invariably equated with the rights of the Estates, which were thereby considered to be supreme in all respects.[33] The right of use was simply the power of the prince to carry on the government, according to prescribed conditions, when the Estates were not in session. The distinction in this form was ideally suited to that dualistic concept of the state which is characteristic of monarchomach theory. It was in this sense that the distinction between ownership and use was most often understood in England.[34]

But in the first quarter of the seventeenth century, a more restricted sense of ownership – for which the term 'real majesty' was used – was introduced by certain writers, mostly of the German school, who either favored absolutism or were willing at least to admit that absolute monarchy was a legitimate form of government. Absolute monarchy, in this conception, meant a 'pure' monarchy in that the prince was not required to obtain the consent of the Estates or other council even for major alterations of ordinary law. But even a prince of this description was required to observe certain rules that preserved the form of the regime and guaranteed its legal continuity. The prince, accordingly, was not entitled to alter the law of succession to the throne, or alienate the powers of his office, especially to foreigners. The latter restriction was often extended to debar excessive gifts to individuals of crown domain and other valuable rights.

For Jean Bodin, these *leges imperii*, or fundamental laws on the form of state, were somehow annexed to the crown as

constituted according to law for the safety and well-being of the universal association, and administers the rights of the latter and puts them into execution. For the rights of the universal association and body politic belong to the body of the universal association, or members of the kingdom, by right of property and lordship and it is only by right of use and administration that they pertain to its supreme magistrate to which they are confided by the body of the Commonwealth' (*Politica methodice digesta* (Cambridge, Mass., 1932), ch. XIX, 2–3, p. 159).

[33] See above p. 4.

[34] It appears whenever the principle *rex singulis maior, universis minor* is invoked.

entails.[35] But in the more sophisticated doctrine of the seventeenth century, they were derived from an original act of constitution by the people. Hence even in an absolute monarchy there was a sense in which 'real majesty' resided in the people, or the realm itself, and the power of the prince was merely personal.[36]

This second meaning of ownership and use contains a distinction (not always strictly observed) between constitutional and ordinary law, and for this reason it is superficially similar to Lawson's usage. Lawson, indeed, was one of the relatively few Englishmen of his time who knew the writings of this German school and paid close attention to them.[37] There are occasional statements in them that he must have found suggestive.[38]

[35] Julian H. Franklin, *Jean Bodin and the Rise of Absolutist Theory* (Cambridge, 1973), p. 71.

[36] 'And therefore this majesty of the commonwealth, or real majesty is comprehended in those fundamental laws by which the commonwealth is constituted. . .and on which it rests as on a foundation through common consent. If these are removed, the well-being and order of the Commonwealth, by which it stands and endures, are necessarily overthrown, or the commonwealth, at least, undergoes mutation, or alteration, into another form' (Christopher Besold, *De majestate in genere. . .*, p. 6, in *Operis politici, editio nova* (Strasbourg, 1626)).

[37] To the best of my knowledge Lawson is the only English writer to mention Besold by name. See *Politica*, pp. 55, 193. But I agree with Salmon, who holds that Besold had other English readers also (J. H. M. Salmon, *The French Religious Wars in English Political Thought* (Oxford, 1959), p. 53). I am inclined to think, however, that this circle was confined to the very learned.

[38] I shall quote three statements by way of illustration:

So long as the body of the commonwealth endures, real majesty continues, and it persists even through interregna and revolutions; and so we can call it the foundation of the commonwealth. (*De majestate*, p. 5.)

The majesty of the ruler is thus distinguished from the majesty of the realm as superstructure from foundation (*tanquam fundamentatum a fundamento*). From this it follows that the majesty of the ruler is bound to the majesty of the realm as though to a superior. (*Ibid.* p. 8.)

Although in a [direct] democracy real and personal majesty seem to flow together. . .yet real majesty is not vested in the people in such a way that a majority can legislate anything in conflict with it. Rather,

Nevertheless, the distinction between real and personal majesty was carried through by these writers only for simple forms of state, and mostly for 'pure,' or absolute, monarchies. It was never used effectively to distinguish the right of the community from that of its established representative, and so was never used to resolve the relationships of sovereignty and the problem of resistance in a mixed constitution.

A clear example of this limitation is the work of Christopher Besold, who was the most sophisticated of these German writers, and the one whom Lawson most appreciated. Besold was one of the very few continental writers of the seventeenth century who was able to conceive a mixed constitution in which independently constituted agents either shared the entirety of sovereignty or held separated portions of it. But when Besold describes the relationships of jurisdiction in systems like the German Empire or the Kingdom of Poland he makes no use of the concept of real majesty. He is always thinking of a single sovereignty shared by two or more parties, or – to put it in simplified form – by the prince, on the one side, and the people, or Estates, on the other. 'Real majesty' thus becomes the whole in which king and people share, but which has no subject of its own.[39] If, therefore, the prince should invade the jurisdiction of the Estates, or otherwise transgress the law, there is no final judgment by the people as

if regard is paid to what is just, abrogation of fundamental laws requires the consent of [all] individuals. For fundamental law has the force of a compact and a covenant, for the change of which the agreement of all is necessary. (Ibid. p. 6.)

[39] Real majesty being thus diffused, there are now two independent partners in sovereignty without a common, constituent authority by which the law that coordinates them may be sustained. Sovereignty is thus divided in an illicit way because too radically. Grotius (who makes the same mistake) is correct in describing a mixed system thus conceived as juridically anomalous. *On the Law of War and Peace*, trans. F. W. Kelsey (Oxford, 1925), bk I, ch. III, par. xvii, 1, 2, pp. 123–4. For the variations in the application of the distinction between real and personal majesty in the second sense, see Otto von Gierke, *Natural Law and the Theory of Society*, ed. and trans. Ernest Barker (Boston, 1957), p. 54ff. and notes; Otto von Gierke, *The Development of Political Theory*, trans. Bernard Freyd (New York, 1939), pp. 164–9; and also Salmon, *French Religious Wars*, pp. 53–4.

a separate entity. The two partners now simply meet as parties to a war in order to settle their dispute. Where, says Besold, the powers of the prince have been limited by fundamental law, the ephors of the people may resort to force if he should violate their jurisdiction: 'And unless this is conceded, the fundamental laws are but shadows. By the very nature of the case, every obligation has an action [of law]. Therefore, since there is no civil action here, the law of nations, namely war, comes into play.'[40]

This outcome is even more clearly exemplified in Grotius. He too, at one point, introduces something akin to the distinction between real and personal majesty in Besold's sense.[41] But when he comes to conflict in a mixed constitution, he assimilates the right of resistance to the law of war:

[I]n case the sovereign power is held in part by the king, in part by the people or Senate, force can lawfully be used against the king if he attempts to usurp that part of the sovereign power which does not belong to him, for the reason that his sovereign authority does not extend so far. In my opinion this principle holds, even though it has already been said that the power to make war should be reserved to the king. For this, it must be understood, refers to an external war. For the rest, whoever possesses a part of the sovereign power must possess also the right to defend his part; in case such a defence is resorted to, the king may even lose his part of the sovereign power by right of war.[42]

40 Christopher Besold, *Principium et finis politicae doctrinae...dissertationes duae quarum una praecognita politices proponit, altera de republica curanda agit,* p. 177, in *Operis politici.* This passage and one or two others leads me to conclude that Hunton was familiar with Besold's work.

41 *Law of War and Peace,* bk I, ch. III, par. vi, p. 102. Grotius speaks here of the whole state as the common subject of majesty (*subjectum proprium*). But he makes little or no use of it legally.

42 *Ibid.* bk I, ch. IV, par. xiii, p. 158. This resort to the laws of war rather than constituent authority reflects the dualism mentioned above.

In Hunton the consequence of winner-take-all is disguised, at the cost of other embarrassments, by the assumption that the power of the king is conferred by God directly.

The winner-take-all version is, however, used by the 'Presbyterian engager,' Anthony Ascham, with the express invocation of Grotius' authority (*The Bounds and Bonds of our Public Obedience* (until recently attributed to Francis Rous) London, 1649), pp. 6–8). Ascham somehow feels able to conclude that the legitimacy of the Commonwealth is thus

The great innovation by Lawson, then, was to apply the second distinction between real and personal majesty not only to simple states but to mixed and limited monarchies as well, and to these, indeed, especially. A fully generalized sense of the distinction is the foundation on which the entire civil part of his *Politica* is built. The result, accordingly, is a systematic and comprehensive reconstruction of the theory of sovereignty.

Thus the starting point for the political part of Lawson's treatise is a quasi-Aristotelian idea of the origin of human groups for which he is avowedly indebted to Althusius.[43] The precondition for an organized political community is the natural association of families with families in neighborhoods, and perhaps of neighborhoods with neighborhoods in some 'vicinity of place.' This informal association is initially held together by social impulse and the perception of mutual economic benefits. It becomes a proper political community only when it agrees to institute a government in order to promote its common life, which is in accordance with the will of God. This agreement to agree upon a government requires the free and deliberate consent of all those who will constitute its members: 'This union doth not arise merely from some accident of cohabitation or natural instinct, but from a rational and just consent – *ex juris consensu* says Cicero. For till they be thus united, they cannot be immediately capable of, or *in proxima potentia* to be a commonwealth.'[44]

established by the right of war. In his answer to Ascham on this point, Edward Gee, in a rare deviation, gives up on the principle of royal sacrosanctity, and not only for the sake of argument. He seems to agree that if war can be levied at all by Parliament against a king, it has the right to win if its cause is just. The best he can do by way of reply is to say that the penalty exacted, deposition, was incommensurate with the injury received (*An Exercitation*, pp. 53–6). Once sacrosanctity is given up, any other answer, however, would have directly contradicted resistance short of deposition. One would either have to say that all resort to force was illicit, or else that government could be changed by consent and then go on to argue that the Rump had not obtained it.

We may also note that Lawson states Grotius' thesis (*Politica*, p. 94) without accepting it.

[43] *Politica*, p. 20.
[44] *Ibid.* pp. 16–17.

The association created by agreement is a community (*civitas*) rather than a commonwealth (*respublica*). Since it is not yet an ordered system of subjection and obedience, it is a commonwealth only in potential. But even so, not all the members who belong to the community are equally its members, or its *cives*. Women, children, servants, strangers, certain kinds of vassals, and all other persons whose obligations may be partly determined for them by another, are citizens only imperfectly, or *virtualiter*.[45] They do not have the *jus suffragii*, or right of deciding, and do not participate in the original agreement. Lawson also speaks of persons who are *eminenter cives*. These 'by reason of their descent, estates, parts, noble acts, are not only members but somewhat more, as being fit for honors, offices, and places of power, if once a commonwealth be constructed.'[46] But this should not be taken to suggest that the original community is divided into privileged estates. Differences of rank and power among persons who otherwise are *sui juris* suppose an order of subjection and thus the institution of a commonwealth. But in their capacity as *cives*, or members of the community, all free persons are politically equal. 'There be, amongst others, three inseparable adjuncts of a community, as a community: propriety of goods, liberty of persons, equality of members.'[47] The *eminenter cives*, therefore, may have a moral claim to offices and honors, but not a legal right. When the community acts as a community, the *jus*

[45] 'The lowest rank [those just referred to as citizens *virtualiter* and *diminute*] is of such as are not *sui juris sed sub potestate aliena* [and so not] free and in their own power. To this form are reduced women, children, servants, strangers, whether sojourning, or inhabiting out of their own commonwealth; some kind of tenants or vassals do so much depend upon others that they are not competent members; all these are virtually included in others upon whom they depend' (*ibid*. pp. 24–5).

[46] *Ibid*. p. 25.

[47] *Ibid*. p. 25. 'Liberty of persons there is, because every complete member is *sui juris*, and in no ways bound by the rules of a civil supreme power; and this is more than can be in a state once constituted wherein this liberty is bounded by allegiance and laws; there is equality, for there is no superior or inferior in respect of government because there is no government, no sovereign, no subject. All are fellows, *et socii quatenus socii sunt aequales*...' (*ibid*. p. 26).

suffragii, or right of decision, is the same for all its members. And these include 'all such, as being males of full age, free, independent, have the use of reason and some competent estate. Such freeholders seem to be with us.'[48]

Despite the absence of an order of subjection, the community is a corporate entity which can bind its members by its vote, and it is by this power that it institutes a commonwealth. The decision on the form of government is normally understood by Lawson as the work of representatives specially chosen for that purpose and deciding by vote of a majority, although only after careful and deliberate discussion.[49] With respect to the government thus instituted, all members become *subditi,* or subject. But they continue to be *cives* also. The community is not absorbed within the commonwealth. It retains its corporate identity, and also its capacity to act. Lawson often describes it – perhaps too passively for what he would convey – as the matter on which governmental form has been impressed.[50]

The real majesty, then, or constituent power of the community, by which a commonwealth was originally established, cannot be lost or transferred so long as the community survives.[51] No matter what the form of government, it cannot be legitimately empowered except on condition that it serve the public good, which is an implicit reservation of real majesty. To grant power otherwise would violate the very end of the community, which would be incompatible not only with the law of nature but with the law of God as well.[52] The majesty of

[48] *Ibid.* p. 26.

[49] *An Examination,* pp. 26–7.

[50] The image may, of course, have been suggested by Hobbes' *Leviathan.* On the relation of Lawson's *An Examination* to the *Politica,* see below p. 87.

[51] 'As this real majesty is a power to model a state, so it is always inherent and cannot be separated' (*Politica,* p. 58).

[52] 'A community may give personal majesty upon condition; and by the laws of God cannot give it otherwise' (*ibid.* p. 100). Lawson sometimes says that the power of the ruler is conferred by God. But he clearly means that the community has the power, in accordance with the will of God, to enforce the conditions it has set. Lawson also insists that a king is sometimes chosen by the special designation of God. But this does not necessarily mean that the people do not have, subsequently, the right of real majesty. See *ibid.* p. 82.

government, accordingly, is always personal, or merely ordinary. Even where it originates in unjust conquest, its power does not become legitimate until it obtains the tacit or express consent of the community.[53] At that point its power also becomes personal and ordinary.

Where, therefore, the conditions on which personal majesty is held are flagrantly transgressed, the obligation to obey is terminated, or 'dissolved.' All authority then reverts to the community, which is entitled not only to replace its governors but to change the form of government itself should it find sufficient cause. Real majesty is the power 'quae potest rempublicam constituere, abolire, mutare, reformare...'[54] And

At one point, however, Lawson admits an exception to the principle that real majesty may not be transferred, and that personal majesty must always be granted on condition. He deplores absolute kingship, all the more so since he assimilates it to despotic, or 'herile' monarchies of the 'oriental' type in which, according to the traditional European representation, the subjects are slaves of the ruler. See Melvin Richter, 'Despotism,' *Dictionary of the History of Ideas*, II (New York, 1973), 1–18. For Lawson, then, absolute monarchy is rule without condition and so a denial of real majesty in the community. Yet after some hesitation, he is unwilling to declare it completely illegitimate. The possibility of transferring real majesty is thus reluctantly conceded but with many warnings that a people ought never to do so. See *Politica*, pp. 132–3 and 62.

[53] 'And this consent [of a community to a form of government] whether mediate or immediate, tacit or express, is so necessary that though a people be conquered, yet the victor cannot govern them as men without their consent' (*ibid*. p. 58). Nevertheless, Lawson does not insist that the choice be free. A people may and often must, in the public interest, submit to a conqueror on the best terms they can (*ibid*. p. 83). Despite occasional suggestions to the contrary, the cause of the conqueror need not be just for submission by the people to be binding, and the 'terms' of protection by the new ruler may be submission to absolute monarchy. Perhaps in the latter case the rule is not over the community as 'men,' but Lawson does not explicitly call it illegitimate. I have not considered either this aberration or despotic monarchy at this point. Except for Lawson's positions on mixed monarchy, I have wished to present only the essentials of his political doctrine, from which these are clearly deviations. I might note, however, that Lawson's mood, when he comes to them, is colored by reflections on submissiveness to the providence of God. What he fails to see is that submission to providence need not entail voluntary legitimation of unjust force. See below pp. 84–5.

[54] *Ibid*. p. 57.

that power, being always latent in the community, can always be exercised on just occasion:

> As real majesty is a power to model a state, so it is always inherent and can never be separated; insomuch that when a form of government is dissolved, or there shall be a failure of succession, the power of the sovereign doth devolve unto them by the law of nature; or rather it was always in the people. As the community hath the power of constitution, so it hath of dissolution, when there shall be a just and necessary cause.[55]

As it has been described thus far, the novelty of Lawson's principle is not immediately discernible. Constitutionalist writers of the seventeenth century, the English not excluded, normally held that a political community arises from agreement among adult males of competent estate and that it may delegate authority only on prescribed conditions; many also held that the people could depose the ruler and change the form of government if the prescribed conditions were transgressed. The new element that now appears with Lawson is his emphatic and consistent denial that the powers of real majesty, or constituent authority, can be transferred to a representative assembly as one of its ordinary powers:

> This act [of real majesty], as with us, is above the power of a Parliament, which may have personal, but cannot have this real majesty. For a Parliament doth necessarily presuppose a form of government already agreed on whereby they are made the subject of personal sovereignty. Therefore they cannot alter or take away the cause whereby they have their being, nor can they meddle with the fundamental laws of the constitution, which, if it once cease, they cease to be a Parliament.[56]

Indeed, deliberate alteration of fundamental law by Parliament would not be binding even if the king agreed to it.[57]

The people, acting to change the form of government, would normally make use of Parliamentary forms. But that would not confuse its real majesty with the personal majesty of Parliament. The representatives would then be empowered by special

[55] *Ibid*. p. 58.
[56] *Ibid*. p. 59.
[57] 'The fundamental government could not be dissolved by one king and one Parliament, though they both had agreed to it' (*ibid*. pp. 383–4).

and temporary mandates, and would meet as a convention rather than as a Parliament:

> If the government be dissolved, and the community yet remains united, the people make use of such an assembly as a Parliament to alter the former government, and constitute a new [one]. But this they cannot do as a Parliament, but considered under another notion as the immediate representative of the community, not of a commonwealth. And thus considered the assembly may constitute a government, which Parliament cannot do, which always presupposing the constitution as such can only act in and for the administration.[58]

But the people is not restricted to the ordinary form of its assembly. Where a government has been dissolved, it may empower a body less or more numerous than Parliament in order to reconstitute a regular authority.[59] The decision on procedure would ultimately lie with the members of the county courts, for these, in Lawson's view, were the original political communities from which the national community of England derived by federation.[60] What he seems to have in mind, as the

[58] *Ibid.* p. 59. In this perspective there is a problem of distinguishing a constituent from an ordinary assembly in a direct democracy which Lawson does not consider except perhaps in a cryptic remark in *An Examination*, p. 24, where he says that in a popular state 'the community and [ordinary] sovereign are the same, though in some respect different.'

[59] 'The form of government was first constituted by the community of England, not by the Parliament. For the community and people of England gave both king and Parliament their being, and if they meddle with the constitution to alter it, they destroy themselves, because they destroy that by which they subsist. The community, indeed, may give a Parliament this power to take away the former constitution and to frame and model another, but this they cannot do as a Parliament, but as trusted by the people for such business and work. Nay, they may appoint another assembly of fewer or more to do such a work without them (*ibid.* p. 162).

[60] *Ibid.* pp. 147–8. The idea is expressed more elaborately in the rebuttal of Hobbes. 'I remember I have read in the *Mirror* [*of Justice*] something to this purpose – that in the first constitution of this government of England, in the time of the Saxons, the forty courts of the forty shires or counties set up a king above them, so that he had neither anyone his superior or peer' (*An Examination*, p. 41). Lawson thus believes that this power now resides in the people of the county courts. 'For the sovereign himself hath no right of himself to change the fundamental constitution. Before this can be done, the people must return unto the original state of liberty and to a community, which in England is not a Parliament, but the forty counties' (*ibid.* p. 15).

fit response to a 'disorderly' dissolution of the government, is a spontaneous movement of the *cives* focused on the county courts, which would then agree among themselves as to the most convenient form of a national convention.[61]

By these principles Lawson is able to reconcile the independence of the king in a mixed constitution with the existence of constituent authority. That he should have come to this solution seems even more remarkable when we consider the republican tendency in his account of the English constitution. Writing in the 1650s, he makes many concessions to the thesis that by the ancient and original constitution all the main prerogatives of sovereignty were vested in the House of Commons. Indeed, even when Lawson is demurring, he is so tactful and conciliatory that he often seems to be concurring.

He thus seems tempted to agree that a separate House of Lords was a late and unwarranted corruption of the pristine constitution. He leaves it as an open question as to '[w]hether they [the Peers] have any share in the legislative power or, if they have, whether in the same house or in a distinct house or body with a negative to the Commons or not, [and] [w]hen this transmitting of bills to the House of Lords began, which some say to be after the barons' war. For it was not so at the beginning.'[62] After showing that the peerage is not defined coherently and that antiquarians are not agreed as to when the House of Lords began, he reflects that 'it will be a very difficult thing to rectify or reduce unto the first institution this house as distinct from that of the House of Commons.'[63] Furthermore, the House of Commons, by the wealth and virtue represented

[61] *Politica*, p. 380.
[62] *Ibid*. p. 159.
[63] *Ibid*. p. 160. In the refutation of Hobbes, Lawson at one point summarized various views of the English constitution and says that 'they would be thought to be more rational, who give the legislative power to the Lords and Commons in one house; the judicial to the Lords in a distinct house; and the executive to the king, who was therefore entrusted with the sword both of war and justice.' But Lawson then goes on immediately to add, of this and all the competing views, 'None of these can give satisfaction' (*An Examination*, p. 32).

by its members, is the 'chief part and almost the whole representative' and the 'Peers to them are but inconsiderable.'[64]

But in the last analysis Lawson still holds to the tradition. The independence of the House of Lords, and even its status as the upper house, had been recognized for many centuries without objection. Its equal status is thus established as a precedent until such time as the English people are persuaded otherwise by clear findings of the antiquarians, or decide to abolish or reform the House of Lords by a deliberate act of real majesty.[65]

On the royal power, Lawson's position is even more nuanced and complex. He believes that English kings had almost never claimed a negative voice in legislation and that when they did their acts were irregular and extraordinary and were not received as precedent.[66] Yet even so he manages to hold that the constitution was tripartite, and his proof, ironically enough, is the coronation oath 'corroborare...justas leges.' This surely means, thinks Lawson, that the king's consent to legislation cannot be lawfully withheld, and it would thus appear that the two houses 'may do anything for the good of the kingdom without him which they may do jointly with him.'[67] Yet the term *corroborare* is also proof that the king's consent, which cannot be withheld, nonetheless is indispensable. The reason for it is his independence as a chief executive. 'Yet because laws and judgment are ineffectual without execution, therefore the king, being entrusted with the execution, was required to give his consent, that he might take care of the execution. For to that end was he trusted with the sword...'[68]

Similar reasoning is encountered in the 1640s among Parliamentary publicists like Prynne. But with Lawson the thrust has been reversed. The essential point is that the king's executive authority is a trust which has been independently established by the people and for which he is not accountable to Parliament. His consent to legislation, however formal, is thus the juridical

[64] *Politica*, p. 157.   [65] *Ibid*. pp. 190, 398.   [66] *Ibid*. p. 153.
[67] *Ibid*. pp. 160, 165.   [68] *Ibid*. p. 160.

link between the highest executive and highest legislative power, without which link personal majesty, or ordinary sovereignty, would not be unified in law.

In this sense at least the king is an integral component of the English legislature in which Lawson, following tradition, locates the highest prerogative or ordinary sovereignty. He is also part of it by his usual power to convene the two houses and dissolve them. That power must be exercised according to the law. The king was obligated to assemble the two houses, and to permit them to remain in session, whenever, and for so long as, public convenience and necessity required. But he made that judgment independently in accordance with an independent trust.[69]

Since the executive power of the king was always to be exerted in accordance with the law, even in the intervals of Parliament when its authority was most pre-eminent, Lawson refers to it as only secondary. Personal majesty, in its primary form, belonged only to the King-in-Parliament which was the seat of legislative power and so 'the foundation and rule of all acts of administration.'[70] Furthermore, since the king did not preponderate in Parliament, the mixture of the English constitution could not properly be called monarchical. It was a 'free state' in the republican meaning of that term.[71] The following, then, is Lawson's constitutional formula for England:

There was a power of kings, and also of Parliaments severally, and a power of them jointly considered. We find the real majesty in the people, and personal majesty in king and Parliament jointly, and a secondary personal majesty, sometimes greater sometimes less, in the kings in the intervals of Parliament.[72]

But since the king's authority could not be taken or altered by the Parliament, the government, although not a monarchy, was a genuine mixture of components no one of which could exercise constituent authority. It follows, therefore, that when one branch of such a mixture exceeds its proper jurisdiction and attempts to subvert the constitution, the people's duty of

[69] *Ibid.* pp. 152–3.   [70] *Ibid.* p. 166.   [71] *Ibid.*   [72] *Ibid.* p. 148.

allegiance ceases not only with respect to that offending branch but to the other components of the government as well. On the one hand, no one branch of government, or even two of them, can assume the functions of the other without altering the government from the form in which the people had established it. Yet on the other hand, the government must cease to operate if any one of its major functions were removed. Hence if real majesty belonged only to the people, Lawson's conclusion was inexorable. The personal majesty of a mixed constitution is dissolved entirely upon the default of any of its parts.[73]

Accordingly, when Charles broke off from Parliament in 1642 and prepared for war against it, the government of England was legally dissolved. This is not to deny that the blame lay solely upon Charles. Charles, in Lawson's view, was the aggressor, and his assault of 1642 was but the final phase of a long-standing and settled design against the liberties and religion of the English people.[74] Yet in strictest law there was nothing that the two houses could have done. All the measures of defense that they adopted were extraordinary in the sense of extralegal and irregular:

Some think an ordinary power continued afoot till the members were secluded [in December 1648]; yet there was no such thing. For the two houses could not, according to the ordinary rules, exercise the ordinary powers of the king, though they might use his name and did so contrary to his consent. If they should allege that his power was forfeited and did devolve on them, that would be hard to prove. We know well enough, if it be not in him, where it is. It could not be in them but for the exercise; and in them, for that end, it was an extraordinary way. Some would say that if the king was dead, either naturally or in law, a Parliament must instantly dissolve and be no Parliament, because there was wanting an essential part. The act of continuance could not help them in this case, for it presupposed all the three essential parts. Neither could any particular Parliament enact that there should be a Parliament without all three essential members. If they should make any such act, by a following Parliament it may be repealed, and the parties, in the name of the people of England, called to account for altering the funda-

[73] 'For no laws could warrant the Parliament to act without the king, or the king without the Parliament' (*ibid.* p. 170).
[74] *Ibid.* pp. 172–3.

78

mental government. For we must not favor any particular Parliament so as to wrong all England, or suffer any ill example to be given.[75]

The legal fact of dissolution is sometimes stated in another way. In 1642 the subject was confronted with opposing writs on the militia, one issued by the king, the other by Parliament. The subject obviously could not obey them both, because the writs conflicted. And in strictest law he could not prefer the Parliament above the king or vice versa, since in strictest law neither one of them could act without the other. It followed then that there was no strictly legal way of obeying anyone at all, and that 'as soon as the commission of array on the one side and of the militia on the other were issued out and put in execution, the subjects in strict sense were freed from their allegiance.'[76]

When, therefore, personal majesty was dissolved in 1642, all power reverted to the general community, which was alone entitled to reconstitute a lawful government.

For if the constitution was dissolved, and the personal majesty forfeited, it must devolve unto the people, and no Parliament, or part of Parliament, or any other person but the people could either alter the former government or model a new one. For according to the general principles of government, the right of constitution, alteration, abolition, reformation is the right of real majesty. For if it be not their right, then the people may be bound to subjection without their consent.[77]

This reversion, furthermore, was automatic. It did not require a preliminary finding by the Parliament or any other constituted body since the entire judgment was the people's. Indeed, Parliament, technically speaking, could not have continued long enough to announce the fact of dissolution. But this is not to say that the people might not have acted earlier. They did not have to wait until personal majesty was dissolved by inner conflict. They would have been justified, presumably, in taking the initiative at almost any time since 1628 when Charles'

[75] *Ibid.* pp. 380–1.
[76] *Ibid.* p. 378. See also pp. 170–1, and also p. 371 where the dissolution is said to have begun as soon as the king deliberately forsook the Parliament.
[77] *Ibid.* p. 382.

tyrannies began. Lawson, in any event, wishes that they had acted soon enough in 1641 or early 1642 to prevent a civil war, and laments that they were too divided and confused to do so.[78]

Yet even though the people remained divided and confused, obligation to real majesty was still incumbent on the individual. A community, unlike a government, is not necessarily dissolved by civil war. It continues to exist, and its majesty remains, so long as there is a will and ultimately the capacity among its members to sustain a common government. The English, Lawson thought, had come close to dissolution, but he rightly believed that they had not reached it.[79]

Real majesty thus continuing, it was the duty of a citizen, or *civis*, to work for reconstitution of a lawful government by all rightful means consistent with the public safety. This is the attitude that Lawson has in mind when he speaks of the 'just party' which all Englishmen were required to support.

If the government was dissolved, it will follow that the subjects were freed from their allegiance; yet the allegiance due the community did continue; and everyone was bound to adhere to the just party according to the laws of God, though in so doing they could not observe the laws of men. And whosoever did oppose the just party, did render themselves forever incapable of the benefit of the English protection, and were *ipso facto* enemies of their own country, their own peace and safety.[80]

---

[78] 'If the counties and people of England had not been ignorant and divided, the division of king and Parliament did give them far greater power than they or their forefathers had for many years. But it did not seem good to the eternal, wise, and just Providence to make them so happy' (*ibid.* p. 380).

[79] '[F]itness, capacity, and immediate disposition to a form of civil government [in a community] doth not arise so much from the multitude of the persons, or extent and goodness of their place of habitation, as from their good affections one towards another and the number of just, wise, and eminent persons amongst them who are fit, not only to be the matter of a state, but to model it and order it once constituted. Experience hereof sufficient we have at this day in this nation. For so many and so great are our differences both in judgment and affections, and our several interests so contrary, that the same language, laws, religion, common country cannot firmly unite us together; but we are ready every moment to fly asunder and break in pieces if we were not kept together rather by the sword of an army than by any civil power and policy, or good affection. This is a sad condition, and a just judgment upon us for our sins' (*ibid.* p. 19).

[80] *Ibid.* p. 371.

In the early 1640s the focus of the just party was that section of the Parliament which wanted merely to preserve the constitution, for this was what the English clearly wanted. In this, no doubt, 'they passed above the letter of the law, and followed the rule of equity and reason, and perhaps they had some hope of rectifying the king, and had no intention of altering the form, if they could preserve it and keep it up. But all their wisdom and endeavor could not prevent the judgment that God intended to execute.'[81]

It thus appears that Lawson would justify in equity all that he condemns in law. Yet the difference is more than empty casuistry. Parliament, by invoking constitutional power for its measures, had imported alterations in the form of government which the English were ultimately unwilling to accept. In other words, it had so distorted or confused the legal relationship of king and Parliament as to make conciliation difficult between the Parliamentary party and well-intentioned royalists. It might thus have done better to declare itself a party and the powers that it exercised provisional.[82]

Furthermore, Parliament's insistence that the law continued had led it into tragic blunders. Looking back at least, Lawson concluded that it ought to have settled the government in 1648 without the king's consent. But the Presbyterians, clinging to legality, refused and thereby helped engender a fateful split within the Parliamentary ranks.[83]

Hence in Lawson's judgment the focus of the just party had shifted to the Independents in 1648, since it was they who introduced the Vote of No Addresses and looked forward to a constitutional settlement without the king's consent. Lawson, in 1657, may even have thought that Pride's Purge was justified in order to avert yet another civil war, even though he does not say so. But he surely believed that the removal of Charles I was beneficial in its consequences, although he presumably

[81] *Ibid*. p. 372.
[82] This is a recurrent theme in the *Politica*. See especially pp. 149, 190.
[83] *Ibid*. pp. 180–1. The Presbyterians are also accused here of being too partial to the Scots.

would not approve his trial and execution by an extraordinary court.

But the error of the Independents on which Lawson particularly dwells was their decision to impose a form of government that Englishmen would not accept. He believes, perhaps naively, that the Independents of the Rump could have avoided this result had they not been driven by fanatic zeal. He protests, in any event, that they had pulled down one arbitrary power only to erect another.[84] They had come to that because they gave their allegiance to a particular ideal of government rather than the needs and wishes of the English people.

Hence neither party had always been just, and at no time had either one been just completely. Just only were those who gave these groups but qualified support, and only for so long as they served the nation's interest. Lawson believed that such persons could have been more or less readily identified. 'For in the midst of these bloody distractions and perplexity of minds, there was a *sanior pars*, a rational judicious party, that unfeignedly desired the peace, welfare, and happiness of England.'[85]

With the Interregnum this *sanior pars* – or more precisely the *pars valentior*, or weightier part, of the judicious party – could no longer look to an organized focus of authority for the representation of its aims. But its course was best exemplified for Lawson by those secluded members who returned to the House of Commons after 1648 and those judges who decided, in 1654, to carry on their duties even without any commission from a king.[86] He was well aware that the existing wishes of most Englishmen were better represented by those who held for Charles II and who even wanted his immediate return. But since that wish was patently unreasonable it did not have

[84] 'For to pull down one arbitrary power to erect another and, neglecting the substance of the Protestant religion, to protect sectaries, and erect new models of their own brain, can be no act of fidelity [to the cause of England]' (*ibid.* p. 181).

[85] *Ibid.* p. 383.

[86] Ibid. p. 385.

to be respected.[87] Reasonable only was gradual progress toward restoration of a lawful government. But this was best accomplished 'little by little' within the framework of the new regime.[88] The more sensible part of the well-affected party was thus justified in acting under it.

The one issue that still remains to be considered is the subject's obligations with respect to a usurper. Here a note of criticism must be introduced, for this is the one point on which Lawson's conclusions seem to go beyond what follows from his premises.

Lawson still admits what I believe he held in 1650 – that a conquered people, subject to overwhelming force, is required to submit in order to protect the public interest. Put in religious terms, submission is in accordance with the providence of God. Since the act of submission seems to entail, for Lawson, a binding obligation of allegiance, he is forced to admit that a conquered people could become absolutely subject to despotic rule.[89] But these conclusions seem inconsistent with his views on the original freedom of the *civitas*. There is no reason why a people, no matter how abject its defeat, should be required – or indeed permitted – to abandon every right to recover its freedom in the future. Lawson might have done better to have said that forced submission was provisional, that it could not be given to a conqueror except in the expectation that he would ultimately acknowledge the right of the community, and that

---

[87] 'When I mention the people of England as the primary subject of power and the heir of real majesty, I mean the rational judicial party; for no consent of people that is not rational and agreeable to the laws of God is of any force. And I exclude not only such as are barely members virtually, but all rebels, traitors, and malignant persons...And when many members of a community are insufficient of themselves to judge what is just and good, and many of them perverted, the power remains in *parte sanior aut in parte hujus partis valentiore*; and in those who upon right information shall consent with them. For many who are not able of themselves to judge, yet when they are rightly informed are willing to consent' (*ibid.* p. 383). Lawson earlier notes that even some of the Cavaliers were 'conscientious' persons although their ignorance does not excuse them completely (*ibid.* pp. 173–4).
[88] *Ibid.* p. 385.
[89] See above p. 72 n. 53.

no promise extorted by duress could prejudice its basic right. The community would thus be free to act against a despot whenever its circumstances should become more favorable.

Writing in 1657, Lawson does not describe the English as a conquered nation or advise submission on that ground. He believes rather that the English were so divided and confused that they were held together, and preserved from anarchy, solely by the sword of the usurper. Hence here too submission is required in the public interest, and so also by the will of God. Lawson, indeed, is so impressed by the benign effects of the existing government that he comes close, at least, at one point, to suggesting that seizure of power to preserve a community from dissolution is hardly to be called a usurpation in the strictest sense.

When we do submit, we must not so much look upon the unjust manner of acquiring the power, as at the power itself, which is from God; and we must consider the necessity which Divine Providence hath brought us into, seeing he gives us no opportunity to right ourselves in respect of human titles, or free ourselves from such as we conceive usurpers, under whom we many times enjoy protection, peace, justice, and the Gospel. . . Yet for all of this we must not justify usurpation that is truly and really usurpation; neither must we swallow gudgeons, comply with every party, and sail with every wind, as some are ready to do. Yet on the other hand, we must not be too scrupulous and pretend conscience, and yet make our fancy or some human constitutions our rule, as though they were divine institutions. For some, whilst they refuse either to submit or act under a power in their conceit [i.e. conception] usurped, they become guilty of a more heinous sin, and when they presume they are faithful to some personal majesty, they prove unfaithful to the real, and their own dear country, preferring the interest of some person, or family, or persons before the good of the whole body of the people to whom they owe more than any other. And whosoever will not be faithful unto his own country, cannot be faithful to any form of government, or personal governors.[90]

Yet it does not appear that an individual, or a group of individuals short of a majority, can give submission, even under these conditions, without prejudice to the right of the com-

[90] *Ibid.* p. 366.

munity as Lawson understands it. An individual might collaborate with the usurper in the public interest and might even call upon his fellow citizens to render him legitimate by a free expression of consent. But the essential right of the community, to have any reasonable form of government on which its majority agrees, could not be ceded by the individual through yielding unreserved allegiance in the absence of general consent.

Thus Lawson might have been better advised to have distinguished limited submission, or collaboration, from full submission, or allegiance, and to have accorded his approval only to the first. But given the circumstances as he understood them, he does not explore this notion fully. Firmly persuaded that destruction of the present power would spell disaster for the English, Lawson would not admit the use of force against it, even as a future possibility. We may point out, however, that some sense of the above distinction is suggested by his actual proposals. Lawson's counsel to the adherents of the just party is not so much to make the existing power permanent as to work for peaceful change. In one passage he says that any act of submission should always be taken in this sense.[91] He seems also to distinguish between giving allegiance to the present government and 'acting under it.' And he may have considered that any submission, no matter what its form, always entails a reservation of real majesty, and so a right to work for change at least by peaceful means. The spirit of his counsels, then, implies at least some reservation of allegiance.

[91] 'Seeing some particular government was necessary, and all rational men did agree in this, therefore there was an obligation to subjection, and every particular person was bound to submit unto the present power under which they enjoyed the benefit of laws, and protection from public enemies and private injustice. This is not so to be understood as though everyone or any ought to rest in this extraordinary condition, but to desire and endeavor to restore the first constitution freed from corruption, or some part or degrees of it, and proceed little by little, as God in divine providence shall prepare the people for it, and enable us to introduce and settle it. But still we must prefer the public good before any particular form of government, and seriously consider what is best to be done for the present' (*ibid.* p. 385).

But whatever the problems in his view of usurpation, they do not affect the general quality of Lawson's work. On every other issue, he is rigorously consistent with his premises, and his insights are elaborated carefully. He thus provides a luminous and highly original theory of resistance in a mixed constitution, and the difficulties just considered, do not detract from that achievement.

4
Locke and the Whigs

LAWSON'S CONTRIBUTION to the theory of sovereignty was not to be appreciated widely or even widely read. In the last years of the Protectorate, when its political applications might have been of interest, his thought was only minimally available. A manuscript of the *Politica sacra et civilis* was sent to the printer in 1657 but was lost. By the time Lawson was able to provide another copy and get it into print, the Protectorate was almost at its end.

A few months, or perhaps a year, after he had finished writing the *Politica*, and had circulated the manuscript among his associates, Lawson was persuaded by 'divers learned and judicious friends' to undertake a refutation of Hobbes' *Leviathan*. This second work on politics, *An Examination of the Political Part of Mr. Hobbes his Leviathan*, actually appeared in 1657 and contained the basic elements of his theory of sovereignty. But Lawson, who seems to have found the undertaking irksome and sought to keep it brief, simply rebutted points in Hobbes according to the latter's order of stating them. He did not, therefore, present his doctrine systematically, nor did he include his thoughts on dissolution. Some of his friends had urged him to be fuller in his refutation. But Lawson had not complied, in part 'because I had formerly finished a treatise of civil and ecclesiastical government which, if it had not been lost by some negligence, after the *Imprimatur* was put upon it, might have prevented and made void the political part of Mr. Hobbes; and although one copy be lost, yet there is another, which may become public hereafter.'[1]

[1] *An Examination of the Political Part of Mr. Hobbes his Leviathan* (London, 1657), Preface.

A clear and full presentation of Lawson's contribution thus did not appear in print until the eve of the return of Charles II. But throughout most of the Restoration, the partisans of constitutionalism prudently abstained from public discussion of the issue of resistance, and seem to have explored it little even privately. When they came to do so in the 1680s, the relevance and value of the *Politica sacra et civilis* must have been difficult to see. It was highly academic in its format, and its Latin terminology was uncongenial to the English taste. Its political message was collaboration with the Commonwealth and the Protectorate, which was a phase of recent history that the Whigs were eager to avoid. Along with all of this, moreover, the idea of dissolution was not a notion that the Whigs would care to notice or to understand. It had caused alarm to an old Presbyterian like Baxter, who in this regard typified respectable opinion of the civil wars and Interregnum.[2] And we shall soon see that it would be no less alarming to the Whig leaders of the Glorious Revolution.[3]

Yet Lawson's work was to be of great importance for the development of political ideas because it was taken up by Locke, and through him alone transmitted to the future. For although the *Politica sacra et civilis* was republished in 1689,

[2] 'I am satisfied that all [theories of] politics err which tell us of a *majestas realis* in the people as distinct from the *majestas personalis* in the governors. And though it be true that *quoad naturalem bonitatem et in genere causae finalis*, the king be *universis minor*. . .yet as to the governing power (which is the thing in question) the king is (as to the people) *universis major* as well as *singulis*. For if the Parliament have any legislative power, it cannot be as they are the body, or the people, . . .but it is as the constitution twisteth them into the government. For if once legislation (the chief act of government) be deemed to be any part of government at all, and affirmed to belong to the people, who are no governors, all government will hereby be overthrown,' *Reliquiae Baxterianae*, ed. Matthew Sylvester (London, 1696), Part 1, 41. Parker and Hooker are the only two writers criticized here. But Lawson is presumably included in those who hold for real majesty, and in any event is not distinguished. The term, moreover, is used by Baxter roughly in Lawson's sense. However, his confusion of legislative and constituent authority indicates that he never fully grasped Lawson's doctrine. For other statements of repudiation of appeals to the people, see below p. 128 n. 2.

[3] See below pp. 105ff.

this did not betoken any general interest in its theoretical position. In that year many statements from the past were reissued indiscriminately as long as they favored resistance in some form or another. There were also three pamphlets of 1689, claiming that a dissolution had occurred, which used Lawson's principles and much of Lawson's terminology.[4] But their suggestions and their argument were not received. Locke, accordingly, was the only major writer who understood and appreciated Lawson's principle. He read the *Politica sacra et civilis*, or at least borrowed it, in 1679, just at the time that he was planning a reply to Filmer.[5] Either then or shortly afterwards Locke must have come to recognize its merits. For not only the theory of resistance, but the basic structure of the *Second Treatise* corresponds to Lawson's view of sovereignty.

Locke's similarity to Lawson has been documented by A. H. Maclean, who was apparently the first to point it out.[6] But Maclean, in noting the similarity, does not interpret or explain the peculiarity of the basic position as it appears in either writer. My purpose in this chapter, therefore, is to provide a clearer view of Locke's intentions. I shall try to explain why he adopted Lawson's theory and why this led him to a serious divergence from most of his Whig contemporaries.

When the Whigs returned to the issue of resistance in the 1680s, the position of the 1640s was unattractive and politically embarrassing. The Cavalier Parliament, which had been freely selected and assembled, had solemnly repudiated all the points of constitutional law and theory on which the old position had been based. In 1661 it declared, among other things, that

---

[4] See below p. 100.

[5] John Locke, *Two Treatises of Government*, ed. Peter Laslett (Cambridge, 1960), Introduction, p. 72, n. 33. On Filmer, generally, see Gordon J. Schochet, *Patriarchalism in Political Thought* (New York, 1975). On Filmer as a critic of the antiquity of the House of Commons, see J. G. A. Pocock, *The Ancient Constitution and the Feudal Law* (Cambridge, 1957), pp. 151–6.

[6] A. H. Maclean, 'George Lawson and John Locke,' *Cambridge Historical Journal*, ix, no. 1 (1947), 68–77, and 'The Origins of the Political Opinions of John Locke' (unpublished doctoral dissertation, Cambridge University, 1947), ch. iv and especially appendix ii.

command of the militia was inherently the king's prerogative and that neither house alone nor both of them together could legislate without the king's consent.[7] It also deliberately condemned the distinction between the king's personal and legal will insofar as it could be used to justify resistance. In 1661 the Cavalier Parliament adopted the first of a series of oaths and tests in all of which the subscriber was required to declare, among other things, 'that it is not lawful, upon any pretense whatsoever, to take arms against the king, and that I do abhor that traitorous position of taking arms by his [the king's] authority against his person, or against those that are commissioned by him.'[8] This declaration was never required of the members of Parliament itself. But in 1675 that was only narrowly averted, more through procedural confusion than from decisive rejection of the principle.[9]

These abjurations furthermore could not be simply swept aside. Not only had they been approved and left in force for twenty years; they also corresponded to the settled rejection by the English public of the principle of Parliamentary supremacy. The bulk of the political nation, which had suffered in the Interregnum, would not tolerate anything that pointed to republicanism. They had now concluded, not incorrectly from a certain point of view, that the revolutionary theory of 1649 was but a logical extension of the resistance theory of 1642.[10]

These considerations against invoking Parliamentary supremacy, finally, were particularly strong in 1679–80, when Locke began the *Second Treatise*. The Whigs were then calculating – too optimistically, as it turned out – that Charles II would be finally driven to accept the Bill of Exclusion by the usual forms of Parliamentary pressure.[11] Consistent with this

[7] Cobbett's *Parliamentary History of England*, vol. IV (London, 1809), cols. 219–20. See also David Ogg, *England in the Reign of Charles II* (Oxford, 1967), pp. 197–8.
[8] Cobbett, vol. IV, col. 241.
[9] For the non-resistance test of 1675 see Cobbett, vol. IV, cols. 719ff.
[10] See, for example, John Nalson, *The Common Interest of Kings and Peoples* (London, 1678), pp. 217ff.
[11] J. R. Jones, *The First Whigs: The Politics of the Exclusion Crisis* (London,

strategy, the Whigs had every reason to reassure the Tories and the waverers of their moderation and respectability. Whig intellectuals were accordingly inclined to take their stand upon the constitution as most Englishmen understood it then to operate. An isolated and doctrinaire republican like Algernon Sidney could still insist that the English people were sovereign in Parliament.[12] But Tyrrell and Locke, who were close to the official Whigs, were bound to admit that the king was independent.

Hence in a critical passage of chapter XIII of the *Second Treatise*, 'On the Subordination of Powers in a Commonwealth,' the principle of Parliamentary supremacy, far from being asserted, is emphatically denied:

The *Executive Power* placed any where but in a Person that has also a share in the Legislative, is visibly subordinate and accountable to it, and may be at pleasure changed and displaced; so that it is not the *supream Executive Power* that is exempt from *Subordination*, but the *Supream Executive Power* vested in one, who having a share in the Legislative, has no distinct superiour Legislative to be subordinate and accountable to, farther than he himself shall joyn and consent; so that he is no more subordinate than he himself shall think fit, which one may certainly conclude will be but little.[13]

This denial of supremacy in Parliament, moreover, is not accompanied by any *arrière pensée* as to some latent and overriding trust. That seems clearly excluded by the passage we have quoted, and there is not the slightest hint of it in any other place. But more positive evidence, apart from silence, is

1961), p. 59. On the political ideas of the period, see especially B. Behrens, 'The Whig Theory of the Constitution in the Reign of Charles II,' *The Cambridge Historical Journal*, VII (1941–3), 42–71, and Carolyn Andervant Edie, 'Succession and Monarchy: The Controversy of 1679–1681,' *American Historical Review*, LXX (1964–5), no. 2, 350–70.

[12] For other pamphlets radical in tendency, see Behrens, 'Whig Theory,' pp. 48–9, and also *Vox Populi, or the People's Claim to their Parliament's Sitting* (1681), which holds that a king may not dismiss Parliament until he has remedied grievances. There is, however, no overt assertion that Parliament can act without the king. The tone, although insistent, is similarly restrained in *A Dialogue at Oxford* (1681) and *A Just and Modest Vindication* (London, 1682).

[13] *Two Treatises*, II, par. 152, pp. 414–15.

Locke's admission that there is a sense in which a king of England can be called supreme, or sovereign, within the constitution.

A somewhat clearer idea of what he had in mind can perhaps be gained by considering the roughly similar position of his friend and confidant, Tyrrell. Tyrrell preferred to think of England as a limited monarchy rather than as a mixed constitution composed of three estates 'according to the opinions held during the late wars.'[14] Part of his reason is the theoretical objection against divided sovereignty advanced by Pufendorf, whom Tyrrell much admired. But the deeper, political reason is that the idea of three coordinate estates had been used, and might be used again, to conclude that the two houses might override the king. For Tyrrell, then, all the prerogatives of sovereignty are vested in the king alone, who is bound, however, to exercise them in accordance with a fundamental law. Following Pufendorf again,[15] he notes that a king need not be absolute in order to be called supreme: '[H]e may still be supreme and yet be limited, not by any power superior to his own, but by his own laws (or declared will) which he himself hath made in the assembly of his Estates, and which he cannot alter but by the same form in which they were established.'[16]

Locke, who was less conservative than Tyrrell, continues to maintain that the English constitution was a mixture of coordinate authorities. Yet even so, a king of England, by virtue of his veto, was required to receive commands from none, and by virtue of his executive authority he could give commands to all. He was thus a political authority that acknowledged no superior, and Locke, presumably by way of reassurance to the Tories, is at pains to observe that a king of England is thereby entitled to be called supreme:

In some Commonwealths, where the *Legislative* is not always in being, and the *Executive* is vested in a single Person, who has also a share in

---

[14] James Tyrrell, *Patriarcha non Monarcha* (London, 1681), p. 236. See also pp. 130–1.

[15] Pufendorf, *Law of Nature*, bk VII, ch. VI, 10, pp. 1070–1.

[16] Tyrrell, *Patriarcha non Monarcha*, p. 129. See below p. 95.

the Legislative; there that single Person in a very tolerable sense may also be called *Supream*, not that he has in himself all the Supream Power, which is that of Law-making; But because he has in him the *Supream Execution* from whom all inferiour Magistrates derive all their general subordinate Powers, or at least the greatest part of them; having also no Legislative superiour to him, there being no Law to be made without his consent, which cannot be expected should ever subject him to the other part of the Legislative, *he is* properly enough in this sense *Supream*.[17]

But having thus admitted the independence of the king and denied Parliamentary supremacy, Locke could no longer employ the traditional doctrine of resistance. Tyrrell, after some hesitation, finally avoided the question.[18] But Locke resolved it boldly by adapting Lawson's theory of dissolution. The way for this is already prepared in Locke's account of the origin and nature of government. Throughout these chapters the idea of the community as a legal entity with independent powers of its own is constantly supposed.[19] In chapter XIII, which deals with the subordination of powers in a commonwealth, this power is at last defined. As long as legitimate government endures, legislation is the highest power, and the composition of the legislature defines the form and essence of the commonwealth. But when that power is seriously abused, is reverts to the general community in which constituent power is permanent and overriding. Lawson's distinction between

---

[17] *Two Treatises* II, par. 151, p. 414. Locke was also influenced by Pufendorf, probably via Tyrrell who quotes him at length, but perhaps also directly since Locke bought a copy of his *Law of Nature* in 1680 (*ibid.* Introduction, p. 158). In this passage the use of Pufendorf would be appropriate. But it may be Pufendorf's authority that led Locke astray in the passage previously quoted where he holds that even a supreme executive, if he does not have a veto, is fully accountable to the legislative and may be dismissed at its pleasure. However, so far as England is concerned, the point is moot.

[18] See below p. 95 n. 21.

[19] However, if these chapters are taken alone, and apart from what is explicitly inferred in the later ones, reservation of constituent power could not be automatically supposed. See above, p. 73 and see also Tyrrell, *Patriarcha non Monarcha*, who offers a theory of origins similar to Locke's but does not draw the same conclusion as to reserved constituent authority.

constituent and ordinary power is thus introduced explicitly, although in a more English terminology:

Though in a Constituted Commonwealth, standing upon its own Basis, and acting according to its own Nature, that is, acting for the preservation of the community, there can be but *one Supream Power*, which is *the Legislative*, to which all the rest are and must be subordinate, yet the Legislative being only a Fiduciary Power to act for certain ends, there remains still *in the People a Supream Power* to remove or *alter the Legislative*, when they find the *Legislative* act contrary to the trust reposed in them. For all *Power given with trust* for the attaining an *end*, being limited to that end, whenever that *end* is manifestly neglected, or opposed, the *trust* must necessarily be *forfeited*, and the Power devolve into the hands of those that gave it, who may place it anew where they shall think best for their safety and security. And thus the *Community* perpetually *retains a Supream Power* of saving themselves from the attempts and designs of any Body, even of their Legislators, whenever they shall be so foolish, or so wicked, as to lay and carry on designs against the Liberties and Properties of the Subject.[20]

When, therefore, Locke takes up the question of resistance, in the last two chapters of the *Second Treatise*, he does not invoke the authority of Parliament, or even hint at it. In chapter XVIII, 'Of Tyranny,' he tacitly accepts one essential point in Filmer's critique of mixed constitutions. In a system like the English there can be no final authoritative judge within the constitution. When the king is charged with tyranny, accordingly, neither Parliament nor any court is entitled to settle the dispute. It would therefore seem to follow that every individual who believes that he has been oppressed is permitted to assault the king and to overthrow his government if possible. The result, warned Filmer, would be utter confusion and ultimately anarchy.[21]

20 *Two Treatises*, II, par. 149, pp. 412–13.
21 In one of his most ingenious arguments, Filmer had attempted to show, against Philip Hunton, that in the absence of a final judge within the constitution every dispute must lead to revolution unless either the king or the community (or Parliament) is rendered absolute: 'I demand of him [Hunton] if there be a variance betwixt the monarch and one of the meanest persons of the community, who shall be the judge? For instance, the king commands me, or gives judgment against me. I reply: his commands are illegal, and his judgment not according to law. Who must judge? If the monarch himself judge, then you destroy the frame of the

For Locke, however, a distinction must be drawn between isolated acts of tyranny – or occasional abuses of executive authority that do not disrupt the law in general – and a calculated design to subvert the law and public liberty as such. In the first case use of force against a king is either deflected by law, or else is effectively debarred in practice. Where recourse to appeal is still available the use of force is always premature. But even where all appeals have been exhausted, resort to force may still be circumscribed by law, as it is in the English constitution. Since the king can do no wrong, force may be used against the king's officials, who would execute illegal orders, but not against the king himself.[22]

state and make it absolute, saith our author. . .On the other side, "if any, or all the people may judge, then you put the sovereignty in the whole body, or part of it, and destroy the being of monarchy." Thus our author has caught himself in a plain dilemma. If the king be judge, then he is no limited monarch. If the people be judge, then he is no monarch at all. So farewell limited monarchy; nay, farewell all government if there be no judge' (*The Anarchy of a Limited or Mixed Monarchy*, in Sir Robert Filmer, *The Freeholder's Grand Inquest*. . .(London, 1679), p. 264). The same critique, developed above for limited monarchy, is applied to mixed monarchy on p. 293.

Locke's answer in effect is that there is a final judgment, but it is a constituent power outside of, or underneath, the constitution, rather than internal to it. Tyrrell (*Patriarcha non Monarcha*, pp. 214ff.) not only disapproves revolution for slight infractions, but would not admit that right at all. Since the act of revolution implies some superiority in the people, and since Tyrrell does not distinguish between superiority constituent and ordinary, the act of revolution seems to violate the principle of monarchy. 'For if the people have a right of punishing the king upon any pretense whatever, there is nothing conferred upon him, but the office of the first magistrate in the commonwealth under the name of king, but the royal power will still remain in the people, because (as I have already laid down) all punishment *quatenus*, as such, must proceed from a superior' (*ibid*. p. 137). Hence even where infractions by the king are major and general in consequence, subjects may disobey only passively and petition for redress. 'For I will not suppose a time (in which this nation is not oppressed by a standing army or men of different principles in religion and government) but the subject may find redress, if not at one time, yet at another' (*ibid*. p. 231). Tyrrell has thus left the door ajar for a broader remedy where the misconduct of the king involves an attempt to subvert the constitution altogether. But he does not yet take up this issue. For his later position, after 1689, see below p. 109.

[22] *Two Treatises*, ii, par. 205, p. 450. Tyrrell, who admits punishment of the

In other systems, where royal immunity is not established by a special rule, the individual is technically permitted to use force against the king, but will not often do so:

For if it [tyranny] reach no farther than some private Mens Cases, though they have a right to defend themselves, and to recover by force, what by unlawful force is taken from them; yet the Right to do so wil. not easily engage them in a Contest wherein they are sure to perish; it being as impossible for one or a few oppressed Men to *disturb the Government*, where the Body of the People do not think themselves concerned in it, as for a raving mad Man, or heady Male-content to overturn a well-settled State; the People being as little apt to follow the one, as the other.[23]

This is the one point in which Locke's formulation is awkward and perhaps unfortunate. He is looking for a rule of morality or law that will enjoin a people from initiating civil war upon light or transient causes. But what he actually provides is a mere prediction of how a people is likely to behave. He might have done better to have said that isolated acts of tyranny must be tolerated by the public, with only peaceful protest, in consideration of the peace and good order of society. This qualification was standard, we may note, in the traditional literature of resistance.[24] A king was not to be deposed unless

king's officers only by the courts, would thus seem closer to the non-resistance oaths required after 1661. But Shaftesbury, arguing against the non-resistance test of 1675, had claimed that the principle could not be extended to preclude forcible resistance to imminent illegal acts (see Cobbett, vol. IV, cols. 716–17), and this is the view that Locke takes.

[23] *Two Treatises*, II, par. 208, p. 452.

[24] So, for example, Grotius (*On the Law of War and Peace*, trans. F. W. Kelsey (Oxford, 1925), I, IV, ii, 1, p. 139 and also I, IV, vii, 2, p. 149), whom Locke must have known; the idea is also used by Tyrrell, with whom Locke held many discussions around 1680. I am inclined to think that Locke's refusal to rely on the usual formulation was deliberate, and I would suggest two reasons for his choice. One was that Filmer, discounting Hunton's use of the traditional reservation, held that it would not be observed in practice even if such restriction were consistent with the system. Hence Locke is at pains to show not only that government may not, but will not, be dissolved on slight cause. The other reason is perhaps Locke's profound respect for the individual. He would not deny the right of a person, injured without redress, to defend his right even if Locke thought he ought to fail.

his misconduct was serious, continuing, and incorrigible by admonition.

Locke, nevertheless, is consistent on the central point. Revolution is appropriate where a people is confronted with a calculated design to subvert its constitution and reduce it to a state of servitude. The king, by repudiating law in general, now forfeits not only the immunity that law confers but all of the authority derived from it. The consequence is entire dissolution of the government and a state of war between the king and the community. In the final passage of chapter xviii there is a warning, probably addressed to Charles II, that revolution will occur if the present course of policy continues.[25]

In chapter xix, 'Of the Dissolution of Government,' parts of which were probably written late in the reign of James II, the grounds of dissolution are more particularly defined. One charge against James is that he was attempting to deliver the people 'into the subjection of a foreign power.' This, as we might note, was a cause of forfeiture on almost any theory then current. But the principal charge against James was a clear and persistent attempt to subvert the constitutionally established legislature – in part by suppression and in part by usurpation of its powers. By this attack on its very foundation, the government became dissolved in its entirety, and its authority reverted to the general community.

Locke, finally, is at pains to make it clear that this reversion to the people was complete. The community was now released from all obligation to the former legislature as a whole, or to any part thereof. Indeed, the very right of judging as to when revolution was required belonged to it alone, and not the two houses of Parliament. In the aftermath of revolution, the people was completely free to choose whatever form of government it deemed best suited to its needs. The people, says Locke, was now at liberty 'to provide for themselves, by erecting a new Legislature, differing from the other, by the change of Persons,

[25] Two *Treatises*, II, par. 210, p. 453.

or Form, or both as they shall find it most for their safety and good.'[26]

Locke had thus adopted an adequate solution to the problem of resistance in a mixed constitution. But that solution was not to be generally accepted in the aftermath of 1688 – and not even by his fellow Whigs, who often rejected it explicitly. The question thus arises as to what it was in Locke's solution that the Whigs found unattractive, and why it was that Locke, in turn, was never willing to accommodate his views to theirs. The answer to this twofold question may help us obtain a clearer view of Locke's intentions and the import of his contribution.

Up to a certain point the Whig position moved in parallel with Locke's. The Whigs were no more inclined to invoke Parliamentary supremacy in 1687 and 1688 than they had been in 1680. Appeal to that idea in order to justify resistance would have hardened Tory opposition and frightened off the moderates, and might even have affronted William of Orange, on whom the entire enterprise was pivoted. The Whigs, accordingly, advanced a theory of forfeiture that would justify resistance to a tyrant without denying that a king of England was independent of the Parliament and even supreme within the constitution. James II, on this view, had forfeited his title to allegiance by deliberately attempting to subvert the constitution. By the law of England, to be sure, a king could do no wrong, and by the oaths required in the Restoration he could not be forcibly resisted. But the presupposition of these rules of law was the continuation of the law itself. James, by repudiating English law, had given up the protections that derived from it.

This argument is stated with admirable lucidity in Gilbert Burnet's pamphlet, *An Enquiry into Measures of Submission...*, which was published in Holland in 1687. 'The [term] king...imports a prince clothed by law with the regal prerogative. But if he goes to subvert the whole foundation of the government, he subverts that by which he himself has his

[26] *Ibid.* ii, par. 220, p. 459.

98

power, and by consequence he annuls his own power and then ceases to be king, having endeavored to destroy that upon which his own authority is founded.'[27]

Burnet's pamphlet was not only among the earliest public statements of the Whig position, but it was also quasi-official in its status. It was probably written after consultation with distinguished English emigrés in Holland. And it was surely published with the approval of William of Orange, who arranged to have it printed in several thousand copies, which were then distributed in England.[28] Burnet, indeed, was among the chief intermediaries between William of Orange and the Whigs, for he also translated and partly shaped the Declaration that William issued when he landed on English soil in September 1688.[29] In any event Burnet's pamphlet was typical ideologically. The basic viewpoint is constantly encountered in other Whig pamphlets of the Glorious Revolution and also in the speeches of the more militant Whig members of the Convention Parliament.[30]

The Whigs would thus agree with Locke that James II had forfeited his title by attempting to subvert the constitution. Beyond this, however, the paths of Locke and the Whigs become divergent. For the latter were unwilling to admit that the consequence of James' forfeiture was entire dissolution of the government. The logic of their argument, no doubt, seemed to point to this inexorably. Burnet had even said that James' trespasses were 'such a breaking of the whole constitution that we can no more have the administration of justice, so that it is really a dissolution of the government.'[31]

---

[27] Gilbert Burnet, *An Enquiry into Measures of Submission to the Supreme Authority...*, in *State Tracts...A Further Collection...*(London, 1692), p. 486.

[28] T. E. S. Clarke and H. C. Foxcroft, *Life of Gilbert Burnet* (London, 1907), p. 243.   [29] *Ibid.*

[30] The use of this idea is so widespread that there is no need to distinguish particular statements. I would note however an influential pamphlet, attributed to Robert Ferguson, that closely follows Burnet's *Enquiry*. See *A Brief Justification of the Prince Orange's Descent into England...* (London, 1689).

[31] *Enquiry*, p. 487. The same point is repeated on p. 488. And it is also made

But talk like this was mainly a way of expressing the enormity of James' crimes. Burnet and the official Whigs had not imagined a reversion of power to the people.[32] After James' flight from England, they made no use of this idea as a means of justifying the Convention Parliament. By January 1689, moreover, when the Convention Parliament assembled, this omission could no longer be explained by any failure of imagination. For at this point the thesis of dissolution had already been presented to the Whigs and was now to be studiously ignored.

The main objective of the Whigs, in January 1689, was to establish William of Orange as the king of England in his own right. In order to preserve some measure of dynastic continuity, Mary, who was James' daughter, was to be given conjoint title. If William and Mary had no issue, the crown would pass to Mary's line on William's death. But William was to have title to the kingship for the duration of his life; he was also to have sole authority to exercise its powers.

By what authority, then, could a king of England be deposed and the order of succession altered without a king's consent? In strictest law a revolution had occurred, one that could be terminated legally only by an exertion of constituent authority. And in the three Lawsonian pamphlets of the time, the Convention was advised to justify its acts on the grounds of a dissolution of the government, and reversion of power to the general community. In two of these – which will be taken up below[33] – the theory of dissolution was associated with radical proposals for sweeping constitutional reforms. But one of them at least proposed the principle as a purely technical solution to the legal problem of succession. The author of *Proposals Humbly Offered to the Lords and Commons in the Present*

in another of Burnet's pamphlets that could have been written fairly early in 1687. See *A Letter Containing Some Reflections on his Majesty's Declaration of Liberty of Conscience*, in *State Tracts. . .A Further Collection*, p. 291.

[32] Burnet would expressly repudiate the thesis of dissolution in a larger sense in his *History of His Own Time*, 6 vols. (Oxford, 1883), III, 383–4.

[33] See below pp. 108, 119–20, 122 n. 79.

Convention for Settling the Government was a great admirer of Lawson, whom he cites by name, and understood his doctrine thoroughly.[34] He thus presented the Convention with a *précis* of Lawson's entire theory of sovereignty modified to fit current notions of the constitution.

The Whigs, however, were unable to follow this suggestion, even had they wished to do so. The English political nation, remembering the Interregnum, was ill at ease over the impending breach in dynastic continuity. And the Tories, who expressed these fears,[35] were therefore powerful. They predominated in the House of Lords, were strongly represented in the House of Commons, and had their own alternatives to offer.

One of these, proposed by the 'authentic' Tories, was to leave James II with his title, but to confer the exercise of power on Mary as his regent. This solution was not without its price in common sense, since it required that James be declared mentally incompetent. But it saved dynastic continuity.

The other Tory solution, recommended by the moderates, was to view the acts of James II, and especially his flight from England, as constructive abdication, which would be part of the Whig solution also. For the Tories, however, the consequence of James' 'abdication' was the immediate and automatic succession of his daughter, Mary, as the next in line. The only legal difficulty here was James II's infant son, the pretended Prince of Wales. But if one were willing to accept the contention, originally offered by the Whigs, that the child was supposititious, dynastic continuity could appear to be preserved.

[34] It appears, among other places, in *State Tracts...A Further Collection*, pp. 455–7.

[35] The Tories often professed to believe that alteration of the order of succession by vote of the two houses would become a precedent, and that England would become an elective monarchy, or even a republic. See Cobbett, vol. v, col. 92 for Nottingham's concern, and see the opinions attributed to other Tories in John Dalrymple, *Memoirs of Great Britain and Ireland*, 3 vols (2nd ed. London, 1790), II, Part I, bk VII, p. 274. See also George L. Cherry, 'The Legal and Philosophical Position of the Jacobites,' *Journal of Modern History*, XXII, no. 4 (December 1950), p. 317.

The only cost in common sense was the notion of constructive abdication.

This second Tory alternative was more realistic politically and thus won more support. It was adopted by the House of Lords, and might have ultimately carried the Convention were it not for William's intervention. He let it be known that he would not remain in England as a consort. This was the decisive factor in the Whigs' success.

In the course of the debates, accordingly, the Whigs made every effort to minimize the breach of continuity. Far from invoking dissolution of the government, they would have had it appear that no deposition had occurred, and that the transfer of the crown to William was in accordance with the constitution. For them, as for the Tory moderates, the acts of James II could be taken as an 'abdication.' For the Whigs, however, the result of James' abdication was to leave the office of the kingship 'vacant,' on which account the two houses, assembling without a king – and in that sense only in the form of a convention – were entitled to supply an occupant. This right of supply, in the absence of a legal king, had supposedly been acknowledged in the past. In any event, this action of the two houses, assuming that a 'vacancy' existed, was the only way to avoid disorder and confusion.[36]

Hence, ironically, the idea of dissolution as it had been presented by the pamphleteers was introduced into the debates of the Convention, not by the Whigs, but by the Tories, who occasionally made clever use of it to reveal the inconsistencies and potential dangers of the theory of vacancy. The clearest statement was by the Tory Earl of Nottingham, who showed the Whigs that their interpretation of the legal situation implied the very dissolution they professed to fear. 'And if the head be taken away, and the throne vacant, by what laws or constitutions is it that we retain the Lords and Commons? For they are

---

[36] See John Maynard, in Cobbett, vol. v, cols. 72–3, 89 (*The Debate at Large between the House of Lords and the House of Commons at the Free Conference...in...1688* (London, 1695), pp. 37–8, 39, 104–5); Robert Howard, in *ibid*. cols. 96–8 (*Debate*, pp. 129–39); and Paul Foley, in *ibid*. col. 107 (*Debate*, pp. 172–3).

knit together in their common head; and if one part of the
government be dissolved, I see not any reason but that all must
be dissolved.'[37] But the fullest statement was by the Tory
moderate, Sir Robert Sawyer. Sawyer apparently would admit
that a vacancy existed only in the narrow sense of an abdication
by James and the passage of the crown to Mary. He warned
the Whigs that an 'absolute,' or total, vacancy entailed complete
dissolution of the government, and therewith of the Convention
Parliament itself:

> The gentleman that first moved in this debate, put it [the forfeiture]
> upon 'a demise' [i.e. that James II was 'dead' in law]. 'Devolution'
> and 'abdication' seem to be the same thing called by various authors.
> You have been moved for other words, and in case of 'abdication' it is
> not difficult. As to the next step, there is a great difference between the
> throne being vacant by abdication and dissolution of the government.
> The vacancy of the throne [in the narrow sense] makes no dissolution
> of the government, either in our law or any other. [But] [i]f the govern-
> ment be fallen to the people, which people we are, what do the Lords
> and we here? If it be devolved on the people, we have nothing to do
> here. We are not the people collectively; we are the representatives of
> the people in the three estates of the nation and the king. And our oaths
> of allegiance, which we take before we sit, are to the hereditary succes-
> sion of the crown. The third estate, which is the House of Commons,
> represents the freeholders and burghers, who are not the fourth part of
> the kingdom. If the government be devolved to the people, copyholders,
> leaseholders, all men under 40s. a year are people. What needs the advice
> of the Lords to reduce things to a settlement? Is it not then the right of
> all the people to send representatives, and our sitting under this frame of
> government is void. . .[38]

[37] Cobbett, vol. v, col. 105 (*Debate*, p. 167).
[38] Anchitel Grey (ed.), *Debates of the House of Commons from the year 1667
to the year 1694*, 10 vols. (London, 1769), ix, 21-2 (Cobbett, vol. v, cols.
48-9). I assume that both Sawyer and Nottingham borrowed their legal
arguments from one more of the Lawsonian pamphlets then abroad. The
term 'dissolution' was, of course, long used in English thought. But it had
always been applied non-technically to describe acts of government so
lawless as to destroy the functioning of law. It is in this sense, as we have
seen, that Burnet uses the term. See above, p. 99. The point of the
Lawsonians, however, was that the forfeiture of a king in a mixed constitution technically requires reversion of power to the people. And this is
the use of the idea by Nottingham and Sawyer. I emphasize this derivation
as evidence that the Whigs' silence on this point was deliberate. If the

The Whigs, quite understandably, refused the bait. Most Whig spokesmen simply reiterated the thesis of a vacancy and passed over the objections as dilatory legal quibbling. A few, as if by way of a reply to Sawyer, vehemently denied that there was any defect in Parliament that was based on the forty-shilling freehold;[39] and one agreed that political power, on James' 'abdication,' had in a sense reverted to the people.[40] But even these were in accord that the powers of the people were those of an ordinary Parliament.[41]

When, therefore, Locke's work was finally published, late in 1689, the Whigs were already committed to the notion of a vacancy supplied by Parliament, and Locke's position, insofar as it was noted, was unwelcome. By this time the cause of the

Lawsonian argument was familiar to the Tories, it must have been known to the Whigs as well. I would also note that the Nottingham–Sawyer objection to the Whig thesis appears among Tory pamphleteers as well. One, at least, is *A Letter to a Member of the Convention*, in *A Collection of Scarce and Valuable Tracts* (Somers Tracts), 4 vols. (London, 1748), I, 320–4, whose author believes (pp. 324–5) that the consequence of dissolution would be reversion to a state of nature. The idea is also represented as 'an odd and unwarrantable notion' in a pamphlet included in *A Collection of State Tracts Published on the Occasion of the Late Revolution in 1688 and during the Reign of King William III*, 3 vols. (London, 1705–7), I, 150–62, where it is entitled, perhaps by the editors, *An Answer to a Letter written by a Member of the Convention*. See p. 162. The arch tone of this pamphlet makes it difficult to determine the political coloration of its author.

I would note, finally, that Sawyer, although surely attempting to embarrass the Whigs on 'vacancy,' is perhaps also replying to some writing or some statement. He could have had the Lawsonian pamphlets in mind, and perhaps even a Whig remark on the floor of the Convention that has not been recorded.

39 Treby, in Grey, IX, 13 (Cobbett, vol. V, col. 41); Boscawen, in Grey, IX, 23 (Cobbett, vol. V, col. 50).
40 Howard, in Grey, IX, 20 (Cobbett, vol. V, col. 46).
41 '[I]t is my opinion,' says Robert Howard, 'that there is an abdication of the government, and it is devolved unto the people, who are here in civil society and constitution to save them[selves]' (Grey, IX, 20 (Cobbett, vol. V, col. 46)). The key word here is 'constitution,' which indicates that the people meet as a Parliament. And Howard says (Cobbett, vol. V, col. 50): 'Much is said of the succession; but we are the people; and threaten ourselves by ourselves when the question is asked: shall we dare to choose?' Hence, the government that was 'dissolved' or 'abdicated' was the crown of James II only.

divergence was not so much that the principle of dissolution might seem to question the legal grounds on which the Convention Parliament had acted. In retrospect at least that assembly might have been construed as a national convention with but a modicum of legal artifice. The larger problem was the portent of Locke's doctrine for the future. Received as precedent, it would authorize the people generally, on any subsequent misconduct of their governors – and even of a single king – to reconstitute a government by any procedure they might choose, and to choose what form of government they wished. To admit dissolution as the legal consequence of James' misconduct would thus appear to open a legal path to radical democracy and even social revolution.

Locke's conception was thus rejected by the Whigs, and William Atwood, a particularly influential Whig apologist, even took special precautions to refute it. The main burden of Atwood's treatise on *The Fundamental Constitution of the English Government*, which appeared in 1690, was to show that English Parliaments had inherent power to supply a royal vacancy. At the end of his review of precedent in support of this opinion, he considers, and answers, the objection that the consequence of James' breach of trust was entire dissolution of the government.

But as the men of form are too strict [on the composition of a convention Parliament], others are too loose in their notions, and suppose the consequence of a dissolution of this contract to be a mere [i.e. pure] commonwealth, or absolute anarchy, wherein everybody has an equal share in the government, not only landed men, and others with whom the balance of the power has rested by the constitution, but copy-holders, servants, and the very *faeces Romuli*, which would not only make a quiet election impractical but bring in a deplorable confusion. But this dilemma they think not to be answered:

Either the old form, as under a monarch, remains, or does not. If it does, the late action of the Lords and Commons was irregular. If it does not, all the people are restored to their original rights; and all the laws which fettered them are gone.[42]

[42] William Atwood, *The Fundamental Constitution of the English Government* (London, 1690), p. 100.

Atwood would resolve this dilemma by general considerations on the nature of political society. In every agreement of a people to erect a government, an implicit proviso must be understood (if the constitution in any way permits it) which is intended to avoid a dissolution on the default of a king. Replying to Hobbes on dissolution, Pufendorf had already represented this proviso. According to him, says Atwood quoting,

They who have once come together in a civil society and subjected themselves to a king, since they have made that the seat of their fortunes, cannot be presumed to have been so slothful as to be willing to have their new civil society extinct upon the death of a king, and to return to their natural state and anarchy, to the hazarding the safety now settled. Wherefore when the power has not been conferred on a king by right of inheritance, or that he may dispose of the succession by his pleasure, it is to be understood to be at least tacitly agreed amongst them that presently upon the death of a king they shall meet together, and that in the place where the king fixed his dwelling. Nor can there well be wanting among any people some persons of eminence who for a while may keep the others in order, and cause them as soon as may be to consult the public good.[43]

Pufendorf is thinking of a non-elective but non-proprietary kingship in which the law of succession is uncertain or, in some given circumstance, fails to designate a new incumbent. He is also thinking of a new election by some version of the general community. But Atwood, at the cost of some distortion, would apply this to a vacancy arising from default, and not from failure of a line established by the law. The new election is not by general convention, but by the constituted three estates of Lords Spiritual, Lords Temporal, and Commons – meeting in a special Parliament. In the light of his study of the precedents, he thought this application warranted by English law.

His own solution thus established, Atwood now takes up the thesis of the *Two Treatises of Government*. It was a work that Atwood much admired. He salutes whoever wrote it as 'the author of the best treatises of civil polity which I have met with in the English tongue,'[44] and he professes to agree with it as a

---

[43] *Ibid*. pp. 100–1 (p. 101 is mispaginated as p. 97). See Pufendorf, *Law of Nature*, bk VII, ch. VII, 9, p. 1092.   [44] *Ibid*. p. 101.

statement of general principles. But its anonymous author, he believed, had overlooked a specific point of English law in his theory of dissolution and had failed to apply the proviso that he might have found in Pufendorf. He 'seems not to have attended to the duplicity, or other particular nature of the contract, in relation to the English government,'[45] and for this reason he had dangerously overstated the consequences of a royal vacancy:

[H]e argues that the people are by the monarch's violation of the constitution restored to the state of nature, there being no common judge in that state of war to which his injuries force them. No man who observes how clearly and consistently he always reasons, can believe that he would apply this to such a state of the question as I have shown that our constitution warrants, which depends not upon a single contract between the people, and a prince and his heirs, whom they had set over them, whose authority ceasing, they were to new mold the government, or set up the like, as they saw fit.

But there plainly was a further contract among themselves, to prevent anarchy and confusion, at any time when the throne might be vacant; and by virtue of this contract they have regularly made those elections, which are frequent in our histories, and are authentic precedents for our later proceedings.[46]

Locke, of course, had never held that the consequence of dissolution was always, or even normally, reversion to a state of nature. And to this minor extent the criticism is mistaken. But there are two or three misleading phrases in chapter XIX, par. 219, which Atwood quotes, that had given him a false impression.[47] For Atwood, furthermore, reversion to a state of nature

---

[45] *Ibid.*

[46] *Ibid.* p. 102.

[47] 'This is demonstratively to reduce all to Anarchy, and so effectually to *dissolve the Government*. . .and the People become a confused Multitude, without Order or Connexion. . .' The term 'anarchy' here does not mean a state of nature in the technical sense of a dissolution of the community, and of the common will to have a government. It means only a situation in which each man must (temporarily) fend for himself. The same idea appears in many places in chapter XIX, and it is probably what is meant by the reference in this paragraph to a 'confused Multitude.' It may be noted that the term 'dissolution' was used in English thought in a non-technical sense to describe a persistent course of illegal action that brought about 'anarchical' conditions. Given Atwood's habituation to this usage, his

and reversion to the people were pretty much the same. What he really objects to in the idea of dissolution is the right of the community to choose another form of government. He would not have softened his criticism even had he read Locke more correctly.

Atwood's next remarks remove all doubt as to this inference. He now turns to a short pamphlet entitled *A Letter to a Friend, advising in this Extraordinary Juncture*, which was one of the three pamphlets of this period based on Lawson's theory of sovereignty. Applying Lawson's theory of dissolution to the events of 1689, the author of *A Letter to a Friend* had proposed a general convention of the people, much larger and more representative than what was then envisaged, to remake the government.[48] Treating this pamphlet, Atwood does not miss the point. The author, he observes, 'would argue a necessity of having a larger representative of the people, that the convention may be truly national.'[49] But this danger, Atwood thinks, is obviated by the special agreement of the English people on the mode of handling a royal vacancy.

There is also at least one other major Whig apologetic in which Locke's idea of dissolution is not only ignored but

---

failure to grasp Locke's insistent distinction between dissolution of government and dissolution of society is more understandable.

[48] The full title is *A Letter to a Friend, advising in this Extraordinary Juncture, how to free the Nation from Slavery forever*, Somers Tracts, pp. 337–9. The key passage on dissolution, which Atwood quotes, is as follows: 'All power is originally, or fundamentally, in the people, formally in the Parliament which is one corporation made up of three constituent essentiating parts – Kings, Lords, and Commons – [and] so it was with us in England. When this corporation is broken, when any one essentiating part is lost or gone, there is a dissolution of the corporation, the formal seat of power, and that power devolves on the people. When it is impossible to have a Parliament, the power returns to them with whom it was originally. Is it possible to have a Parliament? It is not possible. The government therefore is dissolved' (p. 338). The author then goes on to say that the coming Convention should be greatly expanded in its size (pp. 338–9), on which point, see below p. 119.

[49] Atwood, *Fundamental Constitution*, p. 102. In an earlier chapter, Atwood cites and quotes approvingly the *Politica sacra et civilis* of 'the judicious Mr. Lawson' (p. 26), but does not note his theory of sovereignty or views on dissolution.

Locke and the Whigs

deliberately rejected. This repudiation, although less flamboyant than Atwood's, is even more remarkable because it came from James Tyrrell, Locke's friend. Although Tyrrell does not cite the *Two Treatises* by name, he often borrows from it in his *Bibliotheca Politica*. We also know from his letters to Locke that he not only admired the work but had correctly guessed its authorship.[50] But in his own interpretation of the revolution, which is perhaps the most comprehensive of the Whig apologies, Tyrrell opts for the theory of vacancy. 'I never affirmed,' he says,

> that subjects had any authority to abdicate or depose their prince; nor hath the Convention assumed any such powers to themselves. What they have done in this affair has not been authoritative, or as taking upon them to call the king to an account for his actions, or to depose him for misgovernment; but only declarative, to pronounce and declare as the representative of the whole nation that by his endeavor to extirpate the Protestant religion and to subvert the fundamental laws and liberties of the kingdom, he had willfully (I do not say willingly) abdicated the government – that is, renounced to govern the kingdom any longer as a lawful king, which I take to be a tacit and implied abdication of it.[51]

The effect of James' actions then was simply to leave the throne without an occupant, and the Convention Parliament had simply filled it up by 'that inherent power which I suppose doth remain in the estates of the kingdom as representatives of the whole nation to bestow the crown on every abdication or forfeiture thereof on such prince of the blood royal as they shall think best to deserve it.'[52]

Having thus restated the official Whig position on the events of 1689, Tyrrell considers the objection that on the supposition

[50] *Two Treatises*, Introduction, pp. 92–3. Tyrrell seems to have become informed as to the authorship from sources other than Locke himself, as Laslett indicates on p. 93. An earlier statement by Laslett to the contrary (p. 18, n. 7) is perhaps an inadvertent slip.
[51] *Bibliotheca Politica, or an Enquiry into the Ancient Constitution of the English Government* (2nd ed. London, 1727), p. 601 (Dialogue 11). The work consists of fourteen dialogues, the first of which appeared in 1691. The edition of 1694, containing thirteen dialogues, may be taken as the first edition.
[52] *Ibid.* p. 639 (Dialogue 12).

of a vacancy, the government of England would have been absolutely dissolved:

> [S]ince there is no legal government without a king, if the throne were really vacant, and that the people might place whom they pleased on it, yet the Convention can have no power to do it as their representatives; since upon your supposed dissolution of the original contract between the king and the people, there was an end of all conventions and Parliaments too. And therefore if a king could have been chosen at all, it ought to have been by the votes of the whole body of the clergy, nobility, and commons, in their own single persons, and not by any council or convention to represent them; since the laws for restraining the election of Parliament-men only to freeholders, are, upon this supposed dissolution of the government, altogether void; and if you say such a way of election is now impossible, I shall do so too.[53]

Tyrrell, then, is fairly clear as to why Locke thought that dissolution followed from a forfeiture. But he is evidently alarmed by the radical potential of Locke's principle, which perhaps explains why he construes it so destructively. He holds, in order to get rid of it, that the act of reconstruction by the people, in the event of dissolution, could not be carried out by representatives. In any event, his theoretical reply is much the same as Atwood's:

> This objection concerning the total dissolution of the government proceeds from a want of your consideration of what the ancient government of England...a testamentary or elective kingdom, where the kings, being often recommended by the testament of the precedent king, were chosen of the royal family...And tho' it is true there can be now no Parliament without a king, according to the present notion and acceptation of that term, ...it is plain that our great Councils often met by their own inherent authority without any king, and preserved the peace of the kingdom till a new king was either chosen or declared. And tho' 'tis true the crown hath long been enjoyed by those who have claimed it by inheritance, yet there is no reason for all that, if the like cases should fall out as have done in former times, why the government should devolve to the mixed multitude now, any more than it did then; since it may be as well supposed that the same tacit contract still continues of maintaining the original constitution of our great Councils, which I have proved to be as ancient as the kingly government itself.[54]

[53] *Ibid.* p. 643 (Dialogue 12).
[54] *Ibid.*

In one form or other Atwood's and Tyrrell's way of defending the thesis of a vacancy appears in almost all Whig writings on this issue of the 1690s and the early eighteenth century.[55] There is no need, for present purposes, to trace the sequence of these pamphlets. But we should perhaps point out that the basic thought was to be officially received, as it were, by Blackstone, in whom it is also associated with an express critique of Locke. The fact of vacancy, says Blackstone, was determined 'in a full Parliamentary convention representing the whole society.'[56] This decision was not only legally correct, but also prudent in that it averted dissolution of the government:

In particular it is worthy [of] observation that the Convention, in this their judgment, avoided with great wisdom the wild extremes into which the visionary theories of some zealous republicans would have led them. They held that the misconduct of King James amounted to an *endeavor* to subvert the constitution; and not to an actual subversion, or total dissolution, of the government, according to the principles of Mr Locke which would have reduced the society almost to a state of nature; would have levelled all distinctions of honor, rank, offices, and property; would have annihilated the sovereign power, and in consequence have repealed all positive laws; and would have left the people at liberty to have erected a new system of state upon a new foundation of polity. They therefore very prudently voted it to amount to no more than an abdication of the government, and a consequent vacancy of the throne; whereby the government was allowed to subsist, though the executive magistrate was gone, and the kingly office to remain, though King James was no longer king. And thus the constitution was kept entire; which upon every sound principle of government must otherwise have fallen to pieces had so principal and constituent a part as the royal authority been abolished, or even suspended.

This single postulatum, the vacancy of the throne, being once estab-

---

[55] As for example in *The Judgment of Whole Kingdoms and Nations* (8th ed. London, 1713), which, originally published in 1709, at the time of the Sacheverell controversy, as *Vox Populi, Vox Dei...*, seems to have been the most influential Whig apology of this period. J. P. Kenyon, 'The Revolution of 1688: Resistance and Contract,' in Neil McKendrick (ed.) *Historical Perspectives, Studies in English Thought and Society in Honour of J. H. Plumb* (London, 1974), pp. 62, 64.

[56] William Blackstone, *Commentaries on the Laws of England* (21st ed. London, 1844), p. 211.

lished, the rest that was then done followed almost of course. For, if the throne be at any time vacant (which may happen by other means besides that of abdication; as if all the royal blood should fail, without any successor appointed by Parliament); if, I say, a vacancy by any means whatsoever should happen, the right of disposing of this vacancy seems naturally to result to the Lords and Commons, the trustees and representatives of the nation. For there are no other hands in which it can so properly be intrusted; and there is a necessity of its being intrusted somewhere, else the whole frame of government must be dissolved and perish. The Lords and Commons having therefore determined this main fundamental article, that there was a vacancy of the throne, they proceeded to fill up that vacancy in such a manner as they judged the most proper.[57]

Locke, then, had adopted a solution to the problem of resistance that alarmed his Whig contemporaries. Anticipating this reaction, he had sought to give them reassurance by observing that peoples are slow and reluctant to change familiar institutions and that the English people, now as in the past, would return to some version of its ancient constitution. Locke, moreover, had not underestimated the need for such assurances. The passage in which they are presented is, significantly, one of the very few in which he drops his convention of avoiding the use of proper names, and refers explicitly to England:

This slowness and aversion in the People to quit their old Constitutions has, in the many revolutions which have been seen in this Kingdom, in this and former Ages, still kept us to, or, after some interval of fruitless attempts, still brought us back again to our old Legislative of King, Lords and Commons: And whatever provocations have made the Crown be taken from some of our Princes Heads, they never carried the People so far, as to place it in another Line.[58]

Yet Locke could not deny that, in the event of dissolution, a more radical choice might be legitimate according to his principles. He could not, therefore, supply the Whigs with the juridical assurance that they wanted.

Why did Locke persist in a position that was so repugnant to the members of his party? Even in 1687 or 1688, when his chapter on dissolution was revised, he must have noted the

[57] *Ibid.* pp. 213–14.
[58] *Two Treatises*, II, par. 223, pp. 462–3.

trend of official Whig opinion as it was expressed in pamphlets like Burnet's. By 1689, when the *Two Treatises* were published, the main outlines of the Whig position had been fixed in the Convention Parliament. In the 1690s, during which time Locke was frequently engaged in editing and re-editing his work, he could not have overlooked the objections to his thesis, for he owned the works of Atwood and Tyrrell.[59] He could have accommodated these objections without too much alteration of his framework. He had only to add a few paragraphs here and there to incorporate some version of the special proviso that Atwood would suggest.

We should also note in passing that Locke's awareness that his thesis was considered dangerous by all, helps to explain not only his decision to conceal his authorship, but his obsessive efforts to make sure that it was not disclosed by friends. Locke appears to have been a hyper-cautious man,[60] and his concern to avoid being identified as the author of a resistance treatise may seem morbid when compared with that of other Whigs.[61] But given the radicalism of the *Second Treatise*, as it was generally understood, he had special reason to be fearful. Had his authorship become widely known even after 1689, he might have been exposed to prosecution and, at the very least, would have suffered damage to his reputation.

Locke, in any event, deliberately adhered to his opinion,[62]

[59] *Ibid.* p. 90, n. 32; John Harrison and Peter Laslett, *The Library of John Locke* (2nd ed. Oxford, 1971), pp. 77, 254.

[60] Maurice Cranston, *John Locke, A Biography* (New York, 1957), Introduction, p. xi. *Two Treatises*, Introduction, p. 18.

[61] Locke's secretiveness in the early 1680s can be explained as prudence, since he was probably involved in some way with the Whig conspiracies of 1682 and 1683. His caution in Holland can also be explained by normal motives, given the activities there of Stuart agents and the general uncertainty of the future. But in 1689 Locke's behavior was unusual. Other authors – e.g. Tyrrell in his *Bibliotheca Politica* – published anonymously since the situation was still somewhat uncertain. But Locke alone made obsessive efforts to keep his authorship of this particular work from being known even informally.

[62] Laslett puts Locke's deliberateness on the final version of the *Two Treatises* as follows: 'Moreover, the knowledge that he worked so hard and so often at his text is also important in itself. We must surely suppose that he meant

even though it was against the tide. He had worked upon his problem carefully from 1679 to 1681. By 1680, he had become thoroughly familiar with acute statements of the dilemmas of resistance in a mixed monarchy by Filmer, by Hunton (whom he knew, at least through Filmer's criticisms), and also by James Tyrrell (in the *Patriarcha non Monarcha*). At that time he had deliberately settled on the solution that he found in Lawson. When, therefore, he was finally confronted with the official Whig solution, he could have found nothing in it to make him change his mind. For the thesis of vacancy was theoretically hopeless, and subsisted only by confusion.

The argument of Atwood, Tyrrell (in the *Bibliotheca Politica*), and most other Whigs comes down essentially to this. The English kingship was originally elective. In the course of time the order of succession had become fixed according to heredity. But this was not to say that the English crown had now become a strict inheritance. No English king was properly possessed of office until he took the oath of coronation and received indications of consent. The kingship, therefore, was residually elective, or 'elective *sub modo*,' in the words of Atwood.[63] So when the office of kingship becomes vacant, as it had in 1689, the two houses, in which the right of election originally existed, were entitled to supply an occupant.

The premises of this argument are perhaps acceptable. But the conclusion of it is a crude *petitio principii*. The question to be settled is whether the two houses could pass over an existing king and his immediate heirs in order to install another on the throne.[64] The answer is that they may do so if they 'find' a

to stand by what he finally approved for us to see' (*Two Treatises*, Introduction, p. 24).

[63] Atwood, *Fundamental Constitution*, p. 72. For this reason Atwood, on p. 101 (mispaginated as p. 97) criticizes Locke for describing the English executive as consisting of a 'single hereditary person.' See *Second Treatise*, II, par. 213, p. 456.

[64] Tyrrell apparently thought that the choice, in the filling of a vacancy, should fall whenever possible on some 'prince of the blood royal,' on the assumption that the original right of election was normally confined to the choice of persons within the ruling dynasty. But this does not alter the theoretical problem.

vacancy. But to find a vacancy in the sense here meant is already to have found that the king and his heirs have been lawfully excluded.[65]

To speak of 'finding vacancies' is to admit, in evasive and passive language, a power in the two houses not only to depose a king but to alter the constitution of the kingship. If this were so, they were supreme within the constitution – which the Whigs would not admit. But if, on the other hand, they had no power to depose, there was no remedy within the constitution, and the consequence of James' conduct was entire dissolution of the government. This too the Whigs would not admit. But their dilemma was disguised from them by verbal subterfuges.

The same may be said, moreover, of Atwood's attempt to

[65] In order to reduce the complications, I have not mentioned the right of Parliament to supply a king where the existing line has become totally extinct. This right (along with the right to institute a regency where the ruler is incompetent) is sometimes used as a legal analogue. Supply of a king, in the very remote possibility that a line is utterly extinct, is admitted as a right of the Estates by almost all continental authorities. But there are two decisive objections to the analogy:

1. Supply where an extinction has occurred in the sense of no known heirs, is not a deposition, and neither is the institution of a regency.
2. In a constitution like the English, which the Whigs admitted to be mixed, extinction of the line should probably cause a dissolution – unless perhaps there are express provisions on procedures for supply. The people, having confided the kingship to a particular family according to a definite rule, would alone be authorized to make a new rule.

I have also seen another view on vacancy, suggested in the early part of 1689, which I have not discussed in the text since it was (for good reason) hardly followed up. The author of *A Word to the Wise for Settling the Government*, in *Twelve Collections of Papers relating to the present Junction of Affairs* (London, 1689), vol. VI, no. 7 would apply the maxim *nemo est haeres viventis* (there is no heir of a living person). On this rule the throne seemed vacant since, although James had forfeited it, he was still alive (VI, no. 7, 22). Burnet, who mentions this argument, seems also to have accepted it. See *History of His Own Time*, III, 356–7. But the rationale of the maxim cited is that the testator remains in control, and is entitled to change his heir, so long as he remains alive. The rule would not apply to succession to the throne. If it did, it would mean that James, still living, retained complete control of the kingship. The Whig lawyers thus did not press this reasoning. But see Maynard, in Cobbett, vol. V, col. 90 (*Debate*, p. 110) and the reply by Nottingham, in *ibid.* cols. 91–2 (*Debate*, pp. 114–15) for an exchange in the Convention Parliament.

solve the problem by introducing a special proviso into the original agreement of the people. The two houses, acting under that proviso, had been entitled to supply a vacancy in order to avoid a dissolution of the government. But the result is the same as we have just described. If the two houses had really been entrusted with the 'finding' and supply of 'vacancy,' they were supreme within the constitution.

The Whigs thus paid a heavy price in logical consistency for refusing to acknowledge constituent power in the people as a legal entity distinct from Parliament. They wished to hold that the king was independent of the two houses in order to account for the mixture of the constitution. They wished also to hold that a king could be removed for cause and that the law of succession could be altered. But they could not combine these two desiderata without admitting that the government had been dissolved.

We may also note in passing that much the same dilemma reappears in Blackstone. He begins by saying that the Convention Parliament met as trustees of society because the consequence of royal misconduct, where the king is independent, could be decided by society alone[66] – which is clearly to suggest that the settlement of 1689 was legally justified on the ground of dissolution. But Blackstone goes on to say that the Convention properly decided that there had been no dissolution but only a vacancy in the office of the kingship, which it was then entitled to fill up[67] – which is to hold, in effect, that the Convention, assembled on the ground of dissolution, then decided there had been none! With the legal grounds thus shifted, the net result is to suggest that the two houses were entitled to 'find a vacancy' and fill it by some sort of regular capacity within the constitution. Blackstone almost says this in so many words.[68] What he should have said is that a national

---

[66] *Commentaries*, p. 211. 'For whenever a question arises between the society at large and any magistrate vested with powers originally delegated by that society, it must be decided by the voice of society itself; there is not upon earth any other tribunal to resort to.'

[67] *Ibid*. p.213.

[68] '[I]f, I say, a vacancy by any means whatsoever should happen [again],

convention, meeting on a dissolution, had decided to reconstitute the government more or less as it had previously operated. But this would have forced him to pay more attention to the dangerous 'principles of Mr. Locke.'

I would propose, then, that Locke held fast to his position mainly to avoid such difficulties. And I would therefore comment that for this and other reasons I do not share the judgment, once widely held, that Locke, in the *Second Treatise*, was loose with definitions and neglectful of consistency in order to arrive at comfortable conclusions. The *Second Treatise* is a rather rigorously argued work, once its premises are granted. An impression of blandness is conveyed because Locke makes no attempt to distinguish his own position from that of other writers whose political objectives were similar to his. Yet subtle and acute distinctions often lie beneath the surface.

There is yet one other motive that helps account for Locke's persistence in his view of dissolution. Not only was he unafraid, in 1689, of a national convention that would assert constituent authority; he positively favored one as a means of enacting constitutional reforms that he considered to be indispensable guarantees of public liberty.

Major institutional changes were wanted by most Whigs of the Convention Parliament. They were genuinely fearful that the attempt of James (and Charles) to subvert the constitution might be repeated, and they introduced a number of proposals to diminish or exclude the danger. By a new triennial act the king would be obliged to summon Parliament more regularly and would also be required to deal with a newly elected House of Commons in no more than three years' time. By new arrangements on the militia, the king would not be entitled to raise an army and keep it in being without Parliamentary consent. And by guaranteeing judges tenure during good behavior

the right of disposing of this vacancy seems naturally to result to the lords and commons, the trustees and representatives of the nation. For there are no other hands in which it can so properly be intrusted; and there is a necessity of its being intrusted somewhere; else the whole frame of government must be dissolved and perish' (*ibid*. p. 21).

he would be less able to control the courts. Partly connected with these measures, although wanted mostly for its own sake, was toleration for Protestant dissenters or at least liberalization of the church.

Such proposals, along with lesser measures, had been under consideration by a committee of the House of Commons even before a decision was reached on succession to the crown.[69] But the Whigs were finally persuaded, by John Somers, not to press for their immediate adoption. A reasonable case could be made that restoration of legality was the first and most urgent need, and there was danger that the house would become enmeshed in all sorts of more particular issues. The Convention thus decided, although not without some reluctance among many of its members, to postpone consideration of reforms until after William had been crowned.[70]

There was, however, a minority of Whigs who strongly preferred the alternative procedure. If reforms were adopted in advance, it would be all the more difficult for William to temporize or ask for modifications. And if he acknowledged them before his installation, in the course of accepting the offer of the throne, the new arrangements would become part of a new political contract between king and people.

Had this procedure been adopted, the proposed constitutional reforms would probably have been presented to William as declarations of intent and understanding, and only later enacted into law, which was the procedure followed for the Bill of Rights. But on the fringe of the minority that wanted this, there was yet another, and presumably much smaller, group that wanted the enactment of all reforms by constituent authority, which seemed to be higher than an act of Parliament yet did not need a king's consent. This procedure had already been contemplated by radical and left-wing Whigs in Holland.

[69] See Cobbett, vol. v, cols. 53ff.
[70] The proposal of Somers was a compromise. The ancient principles of the constitution – including general statements on most of the important constitutional reforms – were stated in the Declaration of Rights, but all particular questions were postponed. See Thomas Babington Macaulay, *The History of England* (3rd ed. London, 1849), II, 655–7.

It is the message, for example, of the Lawsonian pamphlet, *A Letter to a Friend*, which was originally published in Holland. Dated January 5, 1689, it was apparently written several weeks before the Convention met, and it has been attributed to John Wildman – a former Leveller and indefatigable conspirator, but then a left-wing Whig with some connections to William. The form of the pamphlet is an address to the English people generally, and to the members of the forthcoming Convention in particular, 'advising in this extraordinary juncture how to free the nation from slavery forever.' After showing that the government had been dissolved, it comes to the following conclusion:

The government being dissolved, what must the people do? Care must be taken that the government to be erected be such as will perfectly secure us from slavery; and be a fence inviolable to the liberty and property of the people; and the rights of [ordinary] majesty must be therefore lodged with the Parliament. This will be grateful [i.e. pleasing] to the people. The way of doing it must be great, aweful, and august, that none may be able to quarrel [with] it. A national convention made up of the representatives of the community – that the convention may be truly national, and represent the community, it must be larger than a House of Commons ordinarily is. It is the convention that sets up what kind of government it pleases. If they will have a Parliament made up of king, Lords, and Commons, it is sufficient that this convention is so pleased. The power of the convention must be absolute and uncontrollable, accountable to none but God. It gives laws to kings, yes to the whole Parliament, and sets bounds upon it, [that] it shall go so far, and no further. No act of Parliament can be strong enough to move the foundation laid by this Convention. The Convention, therefore, as it has more power than a Parliament, must have a larger body. What think you, therefore, if the first thing done by the approaching convention be the increasing their number? What if they double it? Whether by ordering every market town to send up their representatives, or every hundred, or wapentake, etc. or in some other way – according to the proportion of the people and public payments, as the wise men of this Convention shall judge most practicable – that it may be the grand council of the nation.[71]

This call, of course, would go unheeded. But even then the

[71] Somers Tracts, 1, 338–9. On the attribution to Wildman, see the following note.

Whig radicals did not give up. Accepting the Convention as it stood, they now advised it to enact reforms immediately and by an assertion of constituent authority. In another, but slightly later, Lawsonian pamphlet, which could well have been written by the author of *A Letter to a Friend* and is also attributed to Wildman, the Convention is urged to enact the reforms that we have mentioned and also to eliminate the royal veto. Some of the less urgent matters might be left to an ensuing Parliament. But the author then concludes with a reminder on constituent authority.

As for the several grievances that need redress, and many good things that are wanting to complete the happiness of our kingdom, there may be some foundation laid happily, or preparations made in order thereunto by this Convention. But as belonging to the administration, and being matters of long debate, they are the work more properly of an ensuing Parliament. Only let not the members of this present great assembly forget, that they having so unlimited a power, and the nation such an opportunity – which, as [with] the secular gains, they are never like to see but once, they are more strictly bound in conscience, and in duty to their country, to neglect no kind of thing, which they judge absolutely necessary to the public good.[72]

There can be little doubt that Locke shared much, and possibly

[72] *Good Advice before it be too late, being a Breviate for the Convention*, in Somers Tracts, I, 339–44. (Portions of this pamphlet are reprinted in Gerald M. Straka (ed.) *The Revolution of 1688* (Boston, 1963), pp. 20–4.) The initial attribution of this pamphlet and of *A Letter to a Friend* to Wildman is by C. H. Firth in the *Dictionary of National Biography*. But Firth gives no documentation, and after examining all the sources he mentions in the article that bear on the revolution period I have found none. Maurice Ashley, *John Wildman, Plotter and Postmaster* (London, 1947), makes the same judgment (pp. 277, 300) also without explanation; and he is presumably following Firth. There is no direct evidence to support this attribution. Although Wildman was a member of the House of Commons in the Convention Parliament, and spoke on a number of occasions, the thesis of dissolution is not suggested in any of his recorded interventions. His only radical proposal was that the House of Commons should be prepared to present its claims of public right directly to William without approval of the Lords (Grey, IX, 79–80). But since Wildman was a clever politician, his silence on dissolution may have been purely tactical, and so, given the strength of Firth's authority, and the fact that Wildman is a likely candidate for authorship, I have accepted the attribution, albeit with reservations.

all, of this opinion. He had become something of a conspirator himself in 1682 and 1683,[73] and may have had some connections with supporters in Holland of the Monmouth uprising of 1685,[74] which was shunned by the more moderate Whigs. He was a friend, in Holland, of radical Whigs like Benjamin Furly and Charles Mordaunt,[75] and was apparently regarded as one of them by Burnet.[76] He also seems to have been personally acquainted with Wildman.[77] But the most important point is that Locke made his views on the Convention reasonably clear in a letter to Edward Clarke. The letter is dated February 7, 1689. But since Locke was still in Holland, he was commenting on the work of the Convention as it stood before the decision on succession, and he criticizes its members for not acting as a constitutional convention. The Convention, he complains to Clarke, had

an opportunity offered to find remedies, and set up a constitution that may be lasting, for the security of the civil rights, and the liberty and property of all the subjects of the nation. These are thoughts worthy such a convention as this, which, if (as men suspect here) they think of themselves as a Parliament, and put themselves into the slow method of proceeding usual therein, and think of mending great faults piecemeal, or anything less than the great frame of government, they will let slip an opportunity. . .[78]

Locke, I take it, surely wanted the Triennial Act, alteration of

[73] *Two Treatises*, Introduction, pp. 44-5.
[74] Cranston, *John Locke*, p. 252.
[75] *Ibid.* pp. 280ff., p. 285.
[76] *Ibid.* pp. 285-6.
[77] A letter from Locke's friend, Martha Lockhart, informs him of Wildman's dismissal from the royal court as though Wildman were a mutual acquaintance. See *ibid.* p. 357.
[78] Benjamin Rand, *The Correspondence of John Locke and Edward Clarke* (Cambridge, Mass., 1927), p. 289. Note also a letter to Locke from the wife of Mordaunt, whom Locke would escort back to England at her husband's request. After some flirtatious remarks, she speaks of kings. 'Ours [i.e. James II] went out like a farthing candle, and has given us by this Convention an occasion not of amending the government, but of melting it down and making all new.' She then went on to 'wish you were there to give them a right scheme of government, having been infected by that great man, Lord "tesbury" [Shaftesbury].' Quoted in Cranston, *John Locke*, p. 308.

the militia, tenure of judges on good behavior, and toleration to be voted by constituent authority. Did Locke also wish, slightly earlier, that the Convention should be expanded in its size and made more representative? I am inclined to think he did, since that is consistent with the tone of the last chapter of the *Second Treatise*, and there are no contrary indications elsewhere. And did Locke wish, at least at the time he wrote to Clarke, to see the veto of the king eliminated? Here the evidence in favor is uncertain and is also contradicted by other indications. Thus I am inclined to say that he did not.[79] The only point on which I would insist is that Locke came to look upon his thesis of dissolution and reversion of power to the general community as a means of introducing constitutional change in 1689.[80]

---

[79] Since this step is recommended by hardly any other Whig (and even the author of *Good Advice* is somewhat tentative) there is no reason to assume that he held that view in the absence of some definite indication in his own statements. But I would note that Locke claims to have 'lost,' and in Laslett's judgment deliberately suppressed (*Two Treatises*, Introduction, p. 66), a middle portion of the work which probably dealt with English constitutional history. That missing section might have given definite clues as to what Locke wanted.

We may also ask whether there was any influence by Locke on the three Lawsonian pamphlets, or vice versa. For the *Proposals Humbly Offered*, any connection may be safely ruled out. That pamphlet is very strictly Lawsonian, and it is also conservative in tone. The other two could not have influenced Locke on the basic theoretical-juridical issue of sovereignty, since he had already come to that around 1680. And given Locke's secrecy about his work, we may doubt that the author(s) of these pamphlets saw the *Second Treatise*. The possibility of oral discussions, which cannot be ruled out, is simply too conjectural to be worth exploring without more information on Locke's associations and on the authorship of the pamphlets. I am inclined to think that the author(s) of the latter went back to Lawson, or to a writing based on Lawson, whether or not on Locke's suggestion. In any event, I have called these two pamphlets, as well as *Proposals Humbly Offered*, 'Lawsonian' because the main point in all of them on dissolution is that no one or two branches of the government in a mixed constitution can assume the function of the other, in the event of default, or change the powers of the other. This thought, which is prominent in the *Politica*, is clearly implied, and intended, in the *Second Treatise*, but is not stated in so many words. For the more militant Whigs, this was an interesting issue only in the last two or three months of 1688 and January 1689, and Locke had no special reason to make a point of it.

[80] But, as indicated earlier, Locke was not required by this view to hold that

I would not contend, on the other hand, that desire for constitutional change was Locke's principal motive in advancing the idea of dissolution, or that it was even present to his mind when he began to write the *Second Treatise*. The need for serious constitutional change was something to which he must have come in the dark days of 1682–8. His overriding concern in 1679 and 1680 was simply to find, by way of a reply to Filmer, a theoretically coherent justification of resistance in a mixed constitution. That was sufficient reason for adopting Lawson's view of sovereignty.

Locke's contribution to the theory of sovereignty was thus to adopt and to transmit a principle of resistance consistent with a mixed constitution.[81] He had found the solution ready-made in Lawson. But he put it in a form and language that made it impossible for his own and later generations to ignore the central thesis, even when they found it dangerous. The *Second Treatise*, then, was the actual source through which Lawson's theory of sovereignty was transmitted to the future and finally received.

In its narrowest application this new idea of sovereignty is no longer particularly relevant. There are few major systems now existing in which the chief executive is constitutionally independent of the legislature. Of these the only one that has been long established is the Constitution of the United States, in which the central problem faced by Locke is resolved by other means.

the acts of the Convention Parliament were in any way defective in law, and he was perfectly justified in saying that William had his title 'in the consent of the people' (*Two Treatises*, Preface, p. 171), since that consent was evidenced not only by the vote of the Convention Parliament but by many other expressions of opinion.

[81] I have not attempted, of course, to deal with Locke's political thought as a whole. Among the best of recent treatments is John Dunn, *The Political Thought of John Locke* (Cambridge, 1969), which approaches the exposition of Locke's thought developmentally.

I have not attempted, either, to consider Locke and his predecessors on the separation of powers as an institutional safeguard, within a constitution, against arbitrary actions. On the history of this idea, see W. B. Gwyn, *The Meaning of the Separation of Powers* (New Orleans, 1965), and M. J. C. Vile, *Constitutionalism and the Separation of Powers* (Oxford, 1967).

One decisive change is quadrennial election of the president, which normally prevents exacerbated and protracted conflict with the Congress. The other, of course, is the power of Congress to impeach and to remove a president, which was in part included by the framers in order to avoid the dilemmas that confronted the English in their civil wars. The device, moreover, is theoretically consistent with a mixed constitution. In principle at least it confers no authority on Congress either to change the rule of succession to the presidency or to alter the powers of the office; yet it is a means of removal for serious misconduct. Hence Locke's and Lawson's solution to the problem of removal is no longer required for a mixed constitution.

But in its broader application, their contribution to the theory of sovereignty continues to be fundamental. In resolving the problem of resistance in a mixed constitution, they had introduced, for the first time, a clear and consistent distinction between constituent and ordinary power, which is of universal application.[82] It establishes the principle that no representative body, no matter how democratically elected, may alter constitutional procedures, or freedoms peculiar to the system that are constitutionally reserved to individuals, without the consent of the general community. In one form or another, this principle is now accepted in all constitutionalist systems. Indeed, in an age when almost everyone, formally at least, is committed to constitutional democracy as an ultimate objective, the idea may even appear obvious. But it was not obvious at the beginning of the seventeenth century. It came to be so only with the emergence of general suffrage and a slow transformation in the idea of the duties of a representative toward his constituents.

But the distinction between constituent and ordinary power is not only important as a statement of the right of the community. It is also fundamental for the theory of public law. With Lawson and Locke almost all accumulated confusions in the theory of sovereignty were finally cleared up. If their ideas on constituent authority sometimes seem commonplace today, it is largely because they were a more or less complete and

[82] For anticipations of this principle, see below p. 125.

adequate expression of the constitutionalist theory of sovereignty.

In its widest application, finally, Locke's idea of constituent authority was to become, along with other aspects of his doctrine, an important source for republican and democratic theories. Lawson and Locke were but tepidly republican at best. And their idea of the community is far from democratic in the modern sense. In Lawson expressly, and in Locke by clear implication, the test of membership is roughly equivalent to the forty shilling freehold as it existed in their time. But their conception of the social compact, especially in Locke's more abstract presentation, is egalitarian in format, and could easily be interpreted more generously. It could then be used, as many Whigs of the 1690s feared, to justify the right of the people to reconstruct the representative in order to make it more responsive.

In this respect, of course, Lawson and Locke were anticipated by the Levellers, whose democratic tendencies were more deliberate as well as more advanced.[83] We should note further that the Levellers also anticipated the distinction between constituent and ordinary power. It is clearly implied in the *Agreement of the People*, and is sometimes stated expressly in their pamphlets.[84] I have not taken up these precedents because I

---

[83] An excellent concise account of Leveller political theory is Peter Zagorin, *A History of Political Thought in the English Revolution* (London, 1954), pp. 8–34.

The right of the people to change the form of government is also encountered among radical Independents. But given their need to justify the coup of 1648, their articulation of the principle is less coherent. See, for example, John Goodwin, *Right and Might Well Met* (London, 1649).

[84] The most thoughtful theoretical formulations are by Robert Overton, whose point of view is already indicated by the long title of one of his most important pamphlets, *An Appeal from the degenerate Representative Body, the Commons of England to the Body Represented, the free people in general of the several counties, boroughs, towns, and places within the Kingdom of England and Dominion of Wales*, in Don M. Wolfe (ed.) *Leveller Manifestoes of the Puritan Revolution* (New York, 1944). See esp. pp. 162, 168.

A somewhat similar view also crops up in a moderate, William Ball, who was called to my attention by Richard Tuck. Ball, like Parker

detect no influence of the Levellers on Lawson or on Locke, who come to their conclusions by a different route and in response to different problems. The point, in any event, is that Leveller ideas were not, unfortunately, to have any direct effect on the subsequent tradition. By 1649 the movement was dispersed; and it had not lasted long enough to produce a major treatise, the influence of which could survive the break-up of the party. Hence when republican and democratic reformers of the last third of the eighteenth century looked for sources of authority and inspiration, they returned to Locke's *Two Treatises*.[85]

(*Observations upon Some of His Majesty's Late Answers and Expresses* (2nd ed. London, 1643), p. 8) believed that the English people had reserved certain liberties from Parliament or King-in-Parliament. Ball took the further step of admitting and insisting – somewhat like the Levellers – that the people could resort to force against its representative if Parliament endeavored to suppress its liberties (*De jure regnandi et regni* (London, 1645), p. 13; *The Power of Kings Discussed* (London, 1649), p. 13; and *State Maxims* (London, 1655), p. 24). I am disinclined, however, to consider Ball a predecessor of Lawson and Locke. There is no clear conception of constituent power or any attempt to resolve the problem of resistance in a mixed constitution. Although Ball, as a moderate, accepts the principle of monarchy, he consistently assumes the right of Parliament to use all the power of the state to correct a tyrant-king (*De jure regnandi et regni*, p. 18; *State Maxims*, p. 15). To my knowledge, the only other moderate who admits a right of the people to use force against their representative is Samuel Rutherford (*Lex, Rex* (London, 1644), p. 152). Since Rutherford has no concern with limitations on the Parliament other than a general obligation to pursue the public interest, there is even less suggestion of constituent authority. Nevertheless, there is one passage (p. 417) where the right of a people to change its form of government is mentioned as an abstract possibility.

[85] The neglect of Locke in the early eighteenth century and the revival of interest in the later part of it, is discussed in John Dunn, 'The Politics of Locke in England and America in the Eighteenth Century,' in John W. Yolton (ed.) *John Locke, Problems and Perspectives* (Cambridge, 1969).

APPENDIX I

On the dating of Lawson's theoretical insight into dissolution

I have assumed that Lawson came to his idea of dissolution somewhere between 1654 and 1656. But there are two other possibilities that cannot be ruled out even though I consider them less plausible for reasons to be presented here. One alternative is that Lawson came to this idea as early as 1642, or at least somewhere before the coup of 1648. The other is that he came to it somewhere around 1650, when he was thinking and writing about the question of allegiance to the Commonwealth.

The first alternative is surely possible. Lawson must have conceived his project for a treatise on ecclesiastical discipline sometime in the 1640s. Comprehension had become a practical possibility. Baxter, furthermore, who was born in 1615, refers to Lawson as an older man. We may thus infer that Lawson (who died in 1678), was about forty when the civil wars broke out, and so mature enough to have become committed to a large-scale program of research and writing. We may also note that Baxter, recalling conversations held with Lawson around 1649, praises him for being 'methodical,' marvels at his 'exact' knowledge of political theory, and credits Lawson with showing him how important the study of political principles was for the understanding of divinity.[1] Lawson, then, was already well

---

[1] After his *Aphorisms of Justification and the Covenants* had been published in 1649, Baxter sent it to clergymen of diverse persuasions for their animadversions. In this context he acknowledges the help he got from Lawson: 'The next animadverter was Mr. George Lawson, the ablest of them all, or of almost any that I know in England – especially the advantage of his age,

read in the theory of public law by 1649. And the terms 'methodical' and 'exact' are associated with the mode of exposition favored by the German school.

But the early 1640s seem an implausible date for Lawson's insight. He would then have been holding a principle that undermined the legal claims of the party that he favored, and put the Parliament, in law at least, on no better footing than the king. Even more important, the principle of dissolution would have frightened a man of Lawson's status. In the circumstances of the 1640s, it would have pointed to a right of rebellion by the people. But the English social and political elite was deeply fearful of any intervention by the people, no matter what the definition of its members. Concern to exorcize that threat is almost universal not only among moderates but among militant adherents of the Commonwealth as well.[2]

It is hard to believe, then, that Lawson would have held a principle that was of little value to his cause and universally repudiated by persons of his social rank. I believe that he had already read Besold. But I suppose that he assumed, somewhat in the fashion of Prynne or Parker, that the people's constituent power could be exerted for them in a crisis by their representatives.[3]

---

and very hard studies, and methodical head, but above all in his great skill in politics [i.e. political science] wherein he is most exact and which contributes not a little to the understanding of divinity' (*Reliquiae Baxterianae*, ed. Matthew Sylvester (London, 1696), I, 107).

[2] Thus Eaton, in reply to Gee's charge that his doctrine invited rebellion by the people: 'I know no such insisted on *in terminis* as he lays down. I know that all wise godly men do abhor such a position of deposing, abolishing their lawful government at pleasure. But that Parliament may do it in the people's name, upon just and weighty causes, is asserted and will be maintained' (*A Reply to an Answer Pretending to Refute Some Positions which Tended to Make the Oath of Allegiance Void and Non-obliging* (London, 1650), p. 39).

[3] We need not assume, however, that any such position on resistance was held by him with any sense of finality or confidence. Lawson, like many others, may have been moved to the side of Parliament more by a sense of equity and necessity, and with only tentative opinions on the basic legal grounds. Baxter, for example, recollecting his own uncertainties as to the rights and wrongs of the contending parties, comments: 'But I then thought that whosoever was faulty, the people's liberties and safety could not be

There is yet another, and less psychological, ground for rejecting this first alternative. But it is best considered in relation to the second which I shall now take up.

The second alternative is not only possible, but has some plausibility, at least initially, in view of those papers on the Engagement that Lawson showed to Baxter. That Baxter says nothing about dissolution in describing them, is no objection, since he also passes over this topic when he describes the *Politica sacra et civilis*. Baxter, I suspect from other passages, never fully grasped this principle as Lawson stated it. In any event the thought of dissolution frightened him, even after 1660.[4] Dating the whole core of Lawson's thought from 1650, furthermore, makes everything much neater, since we then need not suppose an intermediary stage. This is the reason why this view initially attracted me. I clung to it a long time, I must confess, until I finally yielded to accumulating doubts.

The first objection is purely psychological. The idea that dissolution of lawful government occurred in 1642, mitigates the illegality of the coup in 1648 and would thus go hand in hand with favorable expectations from the new regime. For a moderate man like Lawson, that expectation would not have formed, or would not have formed in a decisive way, until the more radical phase of the Commonwealth had passed. I suppose, then, that Lawson's attitude was more like the shocked and dejected mood of whoever wrote *Conscience Puzzled*.

The second objection is only partly psychological since it turns on the publication of the papers seen by Baxter. I assume that Lawson, having written something on the Engagement, would have published it, at least anonymously. But I have read most of the Engagement pamphlets contained in the McAlpin

forfeited. And I thought that all the subjects were not guilty of all the faults of king and Parliament when they defended them: – yea that if both their causes had been bad against each other, yet that the subjects should adhere to that party which most favored the welfare of the nation, and might defend the land under their conduct without owning their cause' (*Reliquiae*, p. 39). Yet at the same time Baxter held a position somewhat similar to that of Hunton and Gee.

[4] See above, p. 88 n. 2.

Collection;[5] I have consulted Wallace's list of Engagement pamphlets for each of which a succinct description is provided; and I have checked with someone who has read still more Engagement pamphlets.[6] Yet for all of this I am aware of no pamphlet of the 1650s that speaks of dissolution in 1642. Assuming that Lawson published what he wrote, the only pamphlet known to me which he might have written would be *Conscience Puzzled*.

In the multitude of pamphlets dating from this period one may yet show up that speaks of dissolution in 1642. I do not expect that this will happen. But if it does I shall cheerfully revise my view. Until such time I shall assume that Lawson's initial position on dissolution was like that in *Conscience Puzzled* and that he later softened and amplified his views for the reasons I have mentioned in the text.

We may note, finally, that this argument from publication is a further objection to the first alternative. If Lawson had come to his ideas of dissolution in the early 1640s, but had decided that publication then would be imprudent, he would nonetheless have the strongest reasons to publish them in 1650. We know from Baxter that he was then in favor of submission. If he could have pointed to a dissolution in 1642, his case for submission would only have been strengthened.

If, therefore, Lawson did not publish his idea of dissolution in 1650, he probably had not come to it in the 1640s. But the converse of this, of course, would not necessarily follow. If it should turn out that Lawson published his idea of dissolution in 1650, one need not assume that he held it in the 1640s. One would, however, want to re-examine that alternative.

[5] At the Union Theological Seminary library, New York City.
[6] Dr Linda Marasco who has just completed a doctoral dissertation at Columbia University on theories of obligation to power *de facto* in this period and at the time of the Glorious Revolution. Cited above p. 62 n. 29.

APPENDIX II

Locke and Burnet

The doctrine and also the language of Burnet's *Enquiry* is often strikingly similar to that of the last two chapters of the *Second Treatise*, especially the second of these chapters. This might lead us to suppose that there was some dependence of Burnet on Locke, as though the latter had shown him portions of the *Second Treatise*, or at least discussed its doctrine with Burnet. The main considerations in support of this hypothesis are these:

Burnet had consistently believed that resistance to a tyrant, although not necessarily wrong in other monarchies, was excluded by the law of England and by the special oaths of submission that had been required after 1661.[1] He did not change his mind until 1686, at which time he would have been in need of sources and suggestions to develop his position. But in 1686 both Burnet and Locke were resident in Holland; both had connections at the Hague; and both were friends of the Dutch theologian, Philip van Limborch. There is also a letter of Locke's which clearly indicates that he was personally acquainted with Burnet.[2] Hence, given the similarities of doctrine and language between the *Enquiry* and the *Second Treatise*, the opportunities for interchange, and Burnet's need for it, the hypothesis of Burnet's borrowing from Locke has some degree of plausibility.

But unless further evidence appears in support of this hypothesis, I am inclined to rule it out. The authors of the standard

---

[1] For Burnet's own account of his earlier position, and the consistency therewith of his later views, see *A Supplement to Burnet's History of My Own Time*, ed. H. C. Foxcroft (Oxford, 1902), pp. 33–8.

[2] Maurice Cranston, *John Locke, A Biography* (New York, 1957), p. 317.

131

biographies of Locke and of Burnet find no evidence of anything approaching friendship or even of extended contact.[3] Locke, as we know, was secretive about all his works, and notoriously so with respect to his *Two Treatises*. Its contents he revealed to hardly anyone. And the very fact of its existence was communicated only to his close friends and confidants, among whom Burnet was not included.

But another objection – which seems to be decisive when connected with the first – is that the idea of forfeiture was available in other sources, and in a form more directly suggestive of the way in which Burnet would actually make use of it. I propose, then – however ironic it may seem at first – that the idea of forfeiture in Burnet, and in the official Whig position generally, went back, via Grotius, to certain absolutist writers of the early seventeenth century, among whom William Barclay and Henning Arnisaeus were most useful.

For these commentators, every monarch who was worthy of that name was absolute. A people, therefore, consistent with the law of God, was not entitled to resist the power of a proper king simply because he was harsh and capricious in his administration of justice, or exacted oppressive tributes from his subjects, or committed any other of the 'ordinary' abuses that were usually cited to justify resistance. But in the extraordinary case of a tyrant–madman like a Caligula or Nero, who openly professes a desire literally to destroy his subjects altogether, both writers were willing to acknowledge an exception – if only because non-resistance pushed to that extreme would make the entire doctrine seem absurd and ludicrous. When, therefore, a king declared open war on his people – or where he alienated his entire power to a stranger – he manifestly renounced the will to govern and his subjects were released from their allegiance.[4]

[3] *Ibid.* p. 285. T. E. S. Clarke and H. C. Foxcroft, *Life of Gilbert Burnet* (London, 1907), p. 228.
[4] William Barclay, *De Regno et regali potestate*...(Paris, 1600) 1, 3, c.8, and Henning Arnisaeus, *De auctoritate principum in populum semper inviolabili* (Strasbourg, 1635), pp. 94–5. In a very qualified way, Arnisaeus admits the possibility of a mixed monarchy (Julian H. Franklin, *Jean Bodin*

Henning Arnisaeus, a German commentator, was little known in England. The same perhaps is true of Barclay also. For although he was a Scot by birth, he emigrated as a result of his Catholicism, and spent most of his career in France. But both of them were used by Grotius, whose work was known not only to Burnet but to almost every educated English commentator. And Grotius succinctly restates the exception of his predecessors in the suggestive language of constructive abdication:

[I]f a king, or any other person, has renounced his governmental authority, or manifestly has abandoned it, after that time proceedings of every kind are permissible against him as against a private person. But he is by no means to be considered to have renounced a thing who is merely too neglectful of it.[5]

I suppose, then, that Burnet and other Whigs found what they were looking for in Grotius and then went back, via his citations, to Barclay, and sometimes to Arnisaeus, if they did not know of these already. One omission, common to these writers, was failure to define the legal situation, or locus of authority, in the aftermath of a 'constructive forfeiture.' Since this case of resistance was but a saving concession on their part, which they never really expected to become actual, they had no need to explore its legal consequences. But precisely by virtue of this oversight, their formulations would have been even more congenial to Burnet. It made it all the easier for him to approach the 'abdication' of James II from the standpoint of a 'vacancy' that left the constitution undisturbed.

Indications of this derivation of the official Whig position are to be encountered everywhere in their speeches and their writings. In Burnet's *Enquiry*, for example, the argument that James II had lost the protection of the law by attempting to destroy it, is finally summarized and clinched as follows:

and the *Rise of Absolutist Theory* (Cambridge, 1973), p. 31) but he does not discuss the issue of resistance in such systems. On familiarity with these writers among English authors see J. H. M. Salmon, *The French Religious Wars in English Political Thought* (New York, 1975), *passim*.
[5] *On the Law of War and Peace*, trans. F. W. Kelsey (Oxford, 1925), bk 1, ch. iv, par. ix, p. 157.

It is acknowledged by the greatest assertors of monarchical power that in some cases a king may fall from his power, and in other cases that he may fall from the exercise of it. His deserting his people, his going about to enslave, or sell them to another, or a furious going about to destroy them, are in the opinion of the most monarchical lawyers such abuses that they naturally divest those that are guilty of them of their whole authority. Infancy or frenzy do also put them under the guardianship of another.[6]

And to take one further illustration, James Tyrrell, in the *Bibliotheca Politica*, not only cites Barclay and Arnisaeus frequently to illuminate his doctrine of resistance, and quotes from them extensively, but quite deliberately insists that the Whig position is a derivation from their premise:

And if this be lawful [i.e. an act of collective self-defense] even in absolute monarchies, the same, I say, may also by the same reason be exercised in limited monarchies, when the king goes about by force to take away the religion, lives, estates, or liberties of the people contrary to a law, since both are founded on the same principle, that a king, by destroying the fundamental laws and constitutions by which he is to govern, renounces the government, and indeed so far dissolves it, that he ceases to be king.[7]

The only problem then remaining was to assimilate James II to a 'frenzied' tyrant like Caligula or Nero. One way, indicated in some of the statements I have quoted, was to construe his attempted subversion of the constitution as a singularly heinous crime. But there was also some tendency to represent James as a vicious monster. From a modern perspective that is gross exaggeration. But in the heated atmosphere of the 1680s it seemed plausible enough to many Whigs.[8]

We should also note, finally, that the invocation of Barclay's opinion is encountered towards the end of Locke's chapter 'Of the Dissolution of Government.' It is barely possible, then,

---

[6] *An Enquiry into Measures of Submission to the Supreme Authority*, in *State Tracts...A further Collection...*(London, 1692), p. 487.

[7] *Bibliotheca Politica* (2nd ed. London, 1727), p. 502. See also William Atwood, *The Fundamental Constitution of the English Government* (London, 1690), pp. 21–2.

[8] Burnet's thought is that only the worst could be expected from a Papist (*Enquiry*, p. 488).

that Locke was initially inspired by this source and then went on, as the Whigs did not, to draw more refined conclusions as to the consequences of a 'forfeiture.' But there are two reasons that lead me to believe that the whole section of this chapter from paragraph 231 through 239 was a late addition. Up to this point the basic argument is dissolution of the government arising from alteration of the legislative power. And then, at paragraph 231, Locke suddenly and belatedly turns to a people's right of collective self-defense, citing Barclay, which is a digression from his central theme and fits in only awkwardly. I also note that some of the language in this section, particularly when Barclay is described, is similar to phrases in Burnet, whose *Enquiry* was published and available to Locke, before his final chapter was rewritten.[9] Locke, then, may well have been borrowing yet another weapon to add to his arsenal of arguments, which he wished to make complete. And of course he would have had every right to do so since the thought is consistent with his general position.

If I am right in this conjecture – and it is hardly more than that – the consequences are ironic. If there was any borrowing between Locke and Burnet, it would be by Locke from Burnet, and not by Burnet from Locke. But whether true or not, of course, the point is minor. Whatever Locke might have borrowed from the *Enquiry* does not affect his basic theory of dissolution in which he sharply diverges from Burnet.

[9] Especially *Second Treatise*, II, par. 232, pp. 467–8, where Barclay is called 'that great Assertor of the Power and Sacredness of Kings,' and, later on, in par. 239, p. 473, 'the great Champion of Absolute Monarchy.'

Bibliography

I. SOURCES

Althusius, Johannes. *Politica methodice digesta*. Cambridge, Mass., 1932.

(Anon.) *An Answer to a Letter written by a Member of the Convention*. In *A Collection of State Tracts...during the Reign of King William III*. 3 vols. London 1705–7. 1, 150–62.

Arnisaeus, Henning. *De auctoritate principum in populum semper inviolabili*. Strasbourg, 1635.

Ascham, Anthony. *The Bounds and Bonds of our Public Obedience*. London, 1649.

Atwood, William. *The Fundamental Constitution of the English Government*. London, 1690.

Ball, William. *De jure regnandi et regni*. London, 1645.

The Power of Kings Discussed. London, 1649.

State Maxims. London, 1655.

Barclay, William. *De regno et regali potestate...*Paris, 1600.

Baxter, Richard. *Reliquiae Baxterianae*, ed. Matthew Sylvester. London, 1696.

Aphorisms of Justification and the Covenants. London, 1649.

Besold, Christopher. *De Majestate in genere...*In *Operis politici, editio nova*. Strasbourg, 1626.

Principium et finis politicae doctrinae...dissertationes duae quarum una praecognita politices proponit, altera de republica curanda agit. In *Operis politici, editio nova*. Strasbourg, 1626.

Blackstone, William. *Commentaries on the Laws of England*. 21st ed. London, 1844.

Bridge, William. *The Wounded Conscience Cured...*London, 1642.

Buchanan, George. *De jure regni apud Scotos* (1578). In *Opera Omnia*, vol. 1. Edinburgh, 1715.

The History of Scotland (1582). Trans. J. Fraser. London, 1689.

Burnet, Gilbert. *History of His Own Time*. 6 vols. Oxford, 1883.

An Enquiry into Measures of Submission to the Supreme Authority. In *State Tracts...A Further Collection...*London, 1692. Pp. 483–8.

Bibliography

A Letter Containing Some Reflections on his Majesty's Declaration of Liberty of Conscience. In *State Tracts...A Further Collection...* London, 1692. Pp. 289–94.

A Supplement to Burnet's History of My Own Time, ed. H. C. Foxcroft. Oxford, 1902.

Burroughs, Jeremiah. *A Brief Answer to Dr. Ferne's Book...* London, 1643.

Clarendon, Edward Hyde, first Earl of. *The History of the Rebellion and the Civil Wars in England.* 6 vols. Oxford, 1888.

Cobbett, William (ed.) *Parliamentary History of England.* 36 vols. London, 1806–20.

A Collection of Scarce and Valuable Tracts (Somers Tracts), 4 vols. London, 1748.

A Collection of State Tracts Published on the Occasion of the Late Revolution in 1688 and during the Reign of King William III. 3 vols. London, 1705–7.

(Anon.) *Conscience Puzzled.* 1650.

The Debate at Large between the House of Lords and the House of Commons at the Free Conference...in 1688. London, 1695.

(Anon.) *A Dialogue at Oxford.* 1681.

Digges, Dudley. *The Unlawfulness of Subjects Taking Up Arms against their Sovereign* (original ed. 1643). London, 1647.

Eaton, Samuel. *The Oath of Allegiance and the National Covenant Proved to be Non-obliging...* London, 1650.

A Reply to an Answer Pretending to Refute Some Positions which tended to Make the Oath of Allegiance Void and Non-obliging. London, 1650.

(Anon.) *England's Apology for its Late Change.* London, 1651.

D'Ewes, Simonds. *The Journal of Simonds D'Ewes from the Recess of the Long Parliament to the Withdrawal of King Charles,* ed. Charles William Havelock Coates. New Haven, Conn., 1942.

Ferguson, Robert. *A Brief Justification of the Prince of Orange's Descent into England...* London, 1689.

Ferne, Henry. *A Reply to Several Treatises.* Oxford, 1643.
The Resolving of Conscience. Cambridge, 1642.
Conscience Satisfied... Oxford, 1643.

Filmer, Sir Robert. *The Anarchy of a Limited or Mixed Monarchy.* In *The Freeholder's Grand Inquest...* London, 1679.

Finch, Henry. *Nomotechnia.* London, 1613.

Franklin, Julian H. *Constitutionalism and Resistance in the Sixteenth Century.* New York, 1969.

Gee, Edward. *An Exercitation Concerning Usurped Powers.* n.p. 1650.
Plea for Non-Subscribers... n.p. 1650.
A Vindication of the Oath of Allegiance... 1650.

Bibliography

Goodwin, John. *Right and Might Well Met*. London, 1649.

Grey, Anchitel (ed.) *Debates of the House of Commons from the year 1667 to the year 1694*. 10 vols. London, 1769.

Grotius, Hugo. *On the Law of War and Peace*, trans. F. W. Kelsey. Oxford, 1925.

Herle, Charles. *A Fuller Answer to a Treatise Written by Dr. Ferne*. London, 1642.

Hunton, Philip. *A Treatise of Monarchy*. London, 1643.

A Vindication of the Treatise of Monarchy. London, 1644.

(Anon.) *A Just and Modest Vindication*. London, 1682.

Lawson, George. *An Examination of the Political Part of Mr. Hobbes his Leviathan*. London, 1657.

Theo-Politica: or a Body of Divinity. . .London, 1659.

Politica sacra et civilis. . .(original ed. London, 1660). 2nd ed. London, 1689.

An Exposition of the Epistle to the Hebrews. London, 1662.

Magna Charta ecclesiae universalis. . .2nd ed. London, 1686.

(Anon.) *A Letter to a Member of the Convention*. In *A Collection of Scarce and Valuable Tracts* (Somers Tracts). London, 1748. I, 320–324.

Locke, John. *Two Treatises of Government*, ed. Peter Laslett. Cambridge, 1960.

(Anon.) *Memorandums of the Conferences Held Between Brethren*. London, 1650.

Nalson, John. *The Common Interest of Kings and People*. London, 1678.

Overton, Robert. *An Appeal from the degenerate Representative Body, the Commons of England to the Body Represented, the free people in general of the several counties, boroughs, towns, and places within the Kingdom of England and Dominion of Wales*. In Don M. Wolfe (ed.), *Leveller Manifestoes of the Puritan Revolution*. New York, 1944.

Parker, Henry. *Observations upon Some of His Majesty's Late Answers and Expresses*. 2nd ed. London, 1643.

A Political Catechism. London, 1643.

Scotland's Holy War. . .as also an Answer to a paper entitled Some Considerations in relation to. . .the Engagement. London, 1651.

(Anon.) *Proposals Humbly Offered to the Lords and Commons in the Present Convention for Settling the Government*. In *State Tracts*. . .*A Further Collection*. London, 1692. Pp. 455–7.

Prynne, William. *The Sovereign Power of Parliaments and Kingdoms*. London, 1643.

Summary Reasons Against the New Oath and Engagement. London, 1649.

Bibliography

Pufendorf, Samuel. *On the Law of Nature and Nations*. Trans. C. H. and W. A. Oldfather. Oxford, 1934.

Rous, Francis. *The Lawfulness of Obeying the Present Government*. London, 1649.

Rushworth, John. *Historical Collections*, 4 vols. London, 1680–92.

Rutherford, Samuel. *Lex, Rex*. London, 1644.

Sanderson, Robert. *Reasons of the Present Judgment of the University of Oxford Concerning the Solemn League and Covenant, the Negative Oath, the Ordinance Concerning Discipline* (1647). In *A Preservative Against Schism and Rebellion...or a Resolution of the Most Important Cases of Conscience Relating to Government Both in Church and State*. London, 1722.

Sheringham, Robert. *The King's Supremacy Asserted*. London, 1660.

State Tracts: A Collection of Several Treatises Relating to the Government. London, 1689.

State Tracts: Being a Further Collection of Several Choice Treatises Relating to the Government. London, 1692.

Twelve Collections of Papers Relating to the Present Junction of Affairs. London, 1689.

Tyrrell, James. *Bibliotheca Politica, or an Enquiry into the Ancient Constitution of the English Government*. 2nd ed. London, 1727. *Patriarcha non Monarcha*. London, 1681.

(Anon.) *Vox Populi, or the People's Claim to their Parliament's Sitting*. London, 1681.

(Anon.) *Vox Populi, Vox Dei...*(1709). Or *The Judgment of Whole Kingdoms and Nations*. 8th ed. London, 1713.

(Wildman, John ?) *Good Advice before it be too late, being a Breviate for the Convention*. In *A Collection of Scarce and Valuable Tracts* (Somers Tracts). I, 339–44.

A Letter to a Friend Advising in this Extraordinary Juncture, How to Free the Nation from Slavery Forever. In *A Collection of Scarce and Valuable Tracts* (Somers Tracts). London, 1748. I, 337–9.

Wolfe, Don M. (ed.) *Leveller Manifestoes of the Puritan Revolution*. New York, 1944.

(Anon.) *A Word to the Wise for Settling the Government*. In *Twelve Collections of Papers Relating to the Present Junction of Affairs*. London, 1689. Vol. VI, no. 7.

(S.W.) *The Constant Man's Character*. London, 1650

II. SECONDARY WORKS

Allen, J. W. *English Political Thought 1603–1644*. London, 1938. *A History of Political Thought in the Sixteenth Century*. London, 1957.

Bibliography

Ashley, Maurice. *John Wildman, Plotter and Postmaster*. London, 1947.

Behrens, B. 'The Whig Theory of the Constitution in the Reign of Charles II,' *The Cambridge Historical Journal*, VII (1941–3).

Benert, Richard Roy. 'Inferior Magistrates in Sixteenth Century Political and Legal Thought.' Unpublished doctoral dissertation, University of Minnesota, 1967.

Bowles, John. *Hobbes and His Critics*. London, 1951.

Cherry, George L. 'The Legal and Philosophical Position of the Jacobites,' *Journal of Modern History*, XXII, no. 4 (December 1950), 309–21.

Clark, T. E. S. and Foxcroft, H. C. *Life of Gilbert Burnet*. London, 1907.

Cranston, Maurice. *John Locke, A Biography*. New York, 1957.

Dalrymple, John. *Memoirs of Great Britain and Ireland*. 2nd ed. London, 1790.

Dunn, John. *The Political Thought of John Locke*. Cambridge, 1969. 'The Politics of Locke in England and America in the Eighteenth Century.' In John W. Yolton (ed.) *Locke, Problems and Perspectives*. Cambridge, 1969.

Edie, Carolyn Andervant. 'Succession and Monarchy: The Controversy of 1678–1681,' *American Historical Review*, LXX (1964–5), no. 2, 350–70.

Franklin, Julian H. *Jean Bodin and the Rise of Absolutist Theory*. Cambridge, 1973.

Gierke, Otto von. *The Development of Political Theory*, trans. Bernard Freyd. New York, 1939. *Natural Law and the Theory of Society*, trans. Ernest Barker. Boston, 1957.

Gwyn, W. B. *The Meaning of the Separation of Powers*. New Orleans, 1965.

Harrison, John and Laslett, Peter. *The Library of John Locke*. 2nd ed. Oxford, 1971.

Hexter, Jack H. *The Reign of King Pym*. Cambridge, Mass., 1961.

Hill, Christopher. *God's Englishman, Oliver Cromwell and the English Revolution*. New York, 1972.

Jones, J. R. *The First Whigs: The Politics of the Exclusion Crisis*. London, 1961.

Judson, Margaret Atwood. 'Henry Parker and the Theory of Parliamentary Sovereignty.' In *Essays in History and Political Theory in Honor of Charles Howard McIlwain*. Cambridge, Mass., 1936. *The Crisis of the Constitution*. New Brunswick, 1949.

Kenyon, J. P. 'The Revolution of 1688: Resistance and Contract.' In

Bibliography

Neil McKendrick (ed.) *Historical Perspective, Studies in English Thought and Society in Honour of J. H. Plumb*. London, 1974. Pp. 43–69.

Macaulay, Thomas Babington. *The History of England*. 3rd ed. London, 1849.

McIlwain, C. H. *Constitutionalism and the Changing World*. Cambridge, 1937.

Maclean, A. H. 'George Lawson and John Locke,' *Cambridge Historical Journal*, IX, no. 1 (1947), 68–77.

'The Origins of the Political Opinions of John Locke.' Unpublished doctoral dissertation. Cambridge University, 1947.

Marasco, Linda. '*De Facto* Obligation: Historical and Theoretical Perspectives.' Unpublished doctoral dissertation. Columbia University, 1977.

Mesnard, Pierre. *L'essor de la philosophie politique au XVIᵉ siècle*. 2nd ed. Paris, 1951.

Ogg, David. *England in the Reign of Charles II*. Oxford, 1967.

Pocock, J. G. A. *The Ancient Constitution and the Feudal Law*. Cambridge, 1957.

'The Political Thought of the Cromwellian Interregnum.' In G. A. Wood and P. S. O'Connor (eds.) *W. P. Morell: A Tribute*. Dunedin, 1973.

(ed.) *The Political Works of James Harrington*. Cambridge, 1977.

Pole, J. R. *The Seventeenth Century: The Sources of Legislative Power*. Charlottesville, 1969.

Rand, Benjamin. *The Correspondence of John Locke and Edward Clarke*. Cambridge, Mass., 1927.

Richter, Melvin. 'Despotism,' *Dictionary of the History of Ideas*. New York, 1973. Vol. II.

Roots, Ivan. *Commonwealth and Protectorate*. New York, 1966.

Salmon, J. H. M. *The French Religious Wars in English Political Thought*. Oxford, 1959.

Schochet, Gordon J. *Patriarchalism in Political Thought*. New York, 1975.

Skinner, Quentin. 'Conquest and Consent.' In G. E. Aylmer (ed.) *The Interregnum*. Hamden, Conn., 1972.

The Foundations of Modern Political Thought, 2 vols. Cambridge, 1978 (forthcoming).

Straka, Gerald M. (ed.) *The Revolution of 1688*. Boston, 1963.

Vile, M. J. C. *Constitutionalism and the Separation of Powers*. Oxford, 1967.

Wallace, John M. 'The Engagement Controversy, 1649–52,' *Bulletin of the New York Public Library*, LXVIII (1964), 384–405.

Bibliography

Weston, Corrine Comstock. *English Constitutional Theory and the House of Lords 1596–1872.* New York, 1970.

Worden, Blair. *The Rump Parliament.* Cambridge, 1974.

Zagorin, Peter. *A History of Political Thought in the English Revolution.* London, 1954.

Index

Index

Cambridge Studies in the History and Theory of Politics

Editors: MAURICE COWLING, G. R. ELTON, E. KEDOURIE, J. G. A. POCOCK, J. R. POLE *and* WALTER ULLMANN

A series in two parts, studies and original texts. The studies are original works on political history and political philosophy while the texts are modern, critical editions of major texts in political thought. The titles include:

TEXTS

Liberty, Equality, Fraternity, by James Fitzjames Stephen. Edited with an introduction and notes by R. J. White

Vladimir Akimov on the dilemmas of Russian Marxism 1895–1903. An English edition of 'A Short History of the Social Democratic Movement in Russia' and 'The Second Congress of the Russian Social Democratic Labour Party,' with an introduction and notes by Jonathan Frankel

J. G. Herder on social and political culture, translated, edited and with an introduction by F. M. Barnard

The limits of state action, by Wilhelm von Humboldt. Edited with an introduction and notes by J. W. Burrow

Kant's political writings, edited with an introduction and notes by Hans Reiss; translated by H. B. Nisbet

Karl Marx's critique of Hegel's 'Philosophy of right,' edited with an introduction and notes by Joseph O'Malley; translated by Annette Jolin and Joseph O'Malley

Lord Salisbury on politics. A selection from his articles in 'The Quarterly Review' 1866–1883, edited by Paul Smith

Francogallia, by François Hotman. Latin text edited by Ralph E. Giesey. English translation by J. H. M. Salmon

The political writings of Leibniz. Edited and translated by Patrick Riley

Turgot on progress, sociology and economics: a philosophical review of the successive advances of the human mind on universal history. Reflections on the formation and distribution of wealth, edited, translated and introduced by Ronald L. Meek

Texts concerning the revolt of the Netherlands, edited and with an introduction by E. H. Kossmann and A. F. Mellink

Georg Wilhelm Friedrich Hegel: lectures on the philosophy of world history: reason in history, translated from the German edition of Johannes Hoffmeister by H. B. Nisbet and with an introduction by Duncan Forbes

A Machiavellian treatise by Stephen Gardiner, edited and translated by Peter S. Donaldson

Regicide and revolution: speeches at the trial of Louis XVI, edited with an introduction by Michael Walzer, translated by Marian Rothstein

STUDIES

1867: Disraeli, Gladstone and revolution: the passing of the Second Reform Bill, by Maurice Cowling

The social and political thought of Karl Marx, by Shlomo Avineri

Men and citizens: a study of Rousseau's social theory, by Judith Shklar

Idealism, politics and history: sources of Hegelian thought, by George Armstrong Kelly

The impact of labour 1920–1924: the beginning of modern British politics, by Maurice Cowling

Alienation: Marx's conception of man in capitalist society, by Bertell Ollman

The politics of reform 1884, by Andrew Jones

Hegel's theory of the modern state, by Shlomo Avineri

Jean Bodin and the rise of absolutist theory, by Julian H. Franklin

The social problem in the philosophy of Rousseau, by John Charvet

The impact of Hitler: British politics and British policy 1933–1940, by Maurice Cowling

Social science and the ignoble savage, by Ronald L. Meek

Freedom and independence: a study of the political ideas of Hegel's 'Phenomenology of Mind,' by Judith N. Shklar

In the Anglo-Arab labyrinth: the McMahon–Husayn correspondence and its interpretations 1914–1939, by Elie Kedourie

The liberal mind 1914–1929, by Michael Bentley

Political philosophy and rhetoric: a study of the origins of American party politics, by John Zvesper

Revolution principles: the politics of party 1689–1720, by J. P. Kenyon